Teaching your child right from wrong

Teaching your child
right
from wrong

by Dorothy K. Whyte

THE **BOBBS-MERRILL** COMPANY, INC.
A SUBSIDIARY OF HOWARD W. SAMS & CO., INC.
Publishers • INDIANAPOLIS • NEW YORK

For my son Michael
with love and thanks

CONTENTS

FOREWORD

This is a book for parents—and for others who work with and care for children and want to teach them right from wrong. It deals with youngsters from their earliest years to their mid-teens.

While ethical values and standards of behavior concern us all, it is important for us as adults to keep in mind that learning right from wrong, as we understand these terms, is a very long-range process for children. A child does not learn ethical behavior as he does a multiplication table, and simply knowing the difference between right and wrong is obviously not enough for him. Our jails are filled with criminals, our hospitals, indeed our streets, with psychopaths who can tell the difference. Parents want to guide their youngsters so that they will not only know the difference, but will usually act on it—so that they will feel right when they do right, wrong when they do wrong.

Ethical development cannot be rushed. What may properly be asked of ten-year-old Janie, for example, is not at all possible for Sally, who has just turned four. But perhaps Bobby, at eleven, should feel a clearer sense of right and wrong than he is currently demonstrating. It is a disservice to him for us not to find out why. Often by not asking enough, or by punishing or rewarding before a child can fully understand, parents impede the progress of ethical development.

Before mothers and fathers can determine what standards to set up, they must have a reasonably accurate picture of what their children can live up to, and what they themselves believe in. Throughout this book the examples of right and wrong and the discussion of general principles are correlated with what can reasonably be expected of a child at specific stages of his growth.

Recently it has become the fashion to assail the amount of child-care advice given to parents and to poke fun at the wealth of newspaper and magazine articles, books and booklets available to them. "Poor, beleaguered parents," runs the current cry at the eagerness with which mothers and fathers seek such information.

This lament impresses us not at all. All of us, new and not-so-new parents alike, are living in times entirely different from those of our grandmothers and grandfathers, or even of our own mothers and fathers. The problem of how to develop ethical behavior in children was complex and never fully solved in their day. The same holds true now, even with our increasing knowledge and understanding of child development. In addition, many of today's parents are uncertain about their own roles in relationship to the ethical behavior of their children. This may be due in part to their reaction against the harsh techniques of an earlier era that were used to teach right and wrong. But this important question still compels our attention, perhaps more so now than ever before. Recurring world crises, the ever-present threat of nuclear destruction, the effects of unprecedented social and economic change at home and throughout the world touch every American family. Is it any wonder that today's parents want to learn more, know more, understand more?

It is naïve to assume that parents accept uncritically all the advice offered them, or that they necessarily feel defeated by conflicting points of view. Just as they know that no two children are alike, so also do they know that no two parents are alike. What some can accept and apply comfortably, others cannot. Mothers and fathers select what seems feasible and possible, and what meets the special needs of their own family. They know that not everything that goes wrong is their fault—or their children's fault. They understand that they will make mistakes, but that those mistakes can be corrected. Out of their reading and their discussions with other parents, they are helped to a deeper understanding of themselves and their children.

All this can serve to strengthen their convictions, enlighten their experiences, modify their attitudes, and lessen their anxieties. Some advance knowledge of what to expect of a child as he grows and develops makes it possible for parents to become more competent and less uncertain—more able to determine when to step in, when to let nature take its course, when to ask for guidance.

When one has been professionally involved in parent education for a number of years, one finds one's own ideas enriched through exposure to those of many colleagues and friends, as well as through the shared experiences of other parents and their children. Many people with whom I have worked—educators, psychiatrists, pediatricians—will recognize in these pages some of their contributions to my thinking. I am deeply grateful to all of them for having added to my knowledge and understanding, not only from their published works but also from our many discussions and conferences over the years.

I want also to thank especially Dr. Lawrence S. Kubie

for his invaluable criticisms; Mrs. Joan W. Parks for her innumerable thoughtful suggestions; Miss Mary Frazee and Miss Eleanor Pasmik, librarians extraordinary; Miss Wendy Bryant and Mrs. Ethel Shiffman for patient and cheerful typing, typing, and retyping.

D.K.W.

Teaching your child right from wrong

Chapter one

THE HOW AND WHY OF

BEING GOOD

At no other time in our history have parents shown more awareness of their responsibilities to their children or tried more conscientiously to meet them than do American mothers and fathers today. Never before has the job been more difficult. No parent, no child can escape completely the anxieties of today's world with its promise of a magnificent future on the one hand and its threat of total annihilation on the other. Questions of good and evil, right and wrong, loom before us with new and compelling force. How to strengthen ethical behavior in ourselves and how to develop it in our children are vital concerns of every parent.

Take Bertha and George Jackson, for example. They are a conscientious, intelligent couple, and their daughter Carol is a happy, lovable six-year-old. For the most part, things run smoothly in their household, although they have the usual ups and downs. Like all parents, they want their child to be good and to grow up to be a good adult. They try to do their best for Carol, but they have misgivings every now and then about how well they actually are doing.

Is happiness enough?

Just the other evening the Jacksons went to a parents' meeting at Carol's school. The subject, "Meeting the Needs of Children," was interesting, the speaker intelligent and thoughtful, and the discussion lively. But talking it all over on the way home, they both owned up to a feeling that somehow something was missing. They were vaguely troubled, without quite knowing why. Finally Bertha Jackson came out with it: "George, I know what it is. I'm a little concerned about all this happiness talk. Of course, we want Carol to be happy, but I also want her to learn right from wrong. Think how important it is. I'm not sure any of us talks about it enough—there must be more to it than loving a child, important though that is."

The Jacksons know, and want to know, much more about the reasons underlying children's behavior than their parents ever did. In common with most mothers and fathers today, they recognize that there are causes for behavior, and that there is a very real connection between how they act and feel and how their children will act and feel. When Carol misbehaves outrageously or gets into a particularly sticky bit of mischief, they don't take the attitude that she was born naughty, and that that's all there is to it. Instead, they want to know the significance of her misbehavior. They wonder if and how it might have been avoided, and whether or not they had contributed to it. They don't go overboard and examine every little action of theirs or Carol's. On the other hand, they know that they are bound to make mistakes, and that all parents do. Still, they prefer not to make too many, nor to leave those they do make uncorrected. They find it helpful to talk things out with other parents. Meetings at Carol's school give them many opportunities to do just that.

But in all the meetings and discussions they had taken part in, only rarely were the words "right" and "wrong" ever mentioned. And that was what bothered Bertha Jackson—it was what was on her mind right now. Speaker after speaker had warned them about being "judgmental," making it seem almost a crime. The Jacksons got the idea that, if not a penal offense, it was at the very least old hat to talk about right and wrong or to express their concern in just those terms. They were a little embarrassed, afraid that they might be considered too strait-laced, not up on modern child-rearing techniques. And they weren't the only ones in that boat. They had plenty of company—other parents concerned, as they were, with teaching their children right from wrong.

What do we mean by right and wrong?

What exactly do we mean by right and wrong—by wanting children to be good and to grow up to be good? Not merely that they be well-mannered, though parents wouldn't mind a touch more of that! Certainly not that they be blindly obedient. Not simply that they stay neat and clean, though that would be fine when it's appropriate. And decidedly not that they remain docile and unquestioning. By teaching children right from wrong, we mean helping them up the slow, gradual path to ethical behavior. And what is ethical behavior based on? On deep feelings of love and sympathy, of justice and fairness, of courage and loyalty.

Does this sound like a tall order? Of course it does. But it is certainly the kind of behavior that parents want their children to develop. Let's look at some simple examples.

Eight-year-old Joe Knight finished only ten of the twelve problems on his arithmetic test. His teacher didn't notice and marked his paper 100. He tells her about it, and the truth brings his mark down to 83. Hilary Stern, thirteen, returns a gold watch she found on the bus, even though no one had noticed her pick it up. Fifteen-year-old Frank Decker defends the rights of minorities in his school, although this position is unpopular in his community. These youngsters are *good*, not "goody-good." They know right from wrong. Their behavior is truly ethical.

Love is not all

Modern parents realize that the antediluvian technique of "spare the rod and spoil the child" is not the way to teach ethical conduct. They know that it is neither kind nor effective nor intelligent. More than that, they have learned that it can be dangerous and damaging. And it has certainly never produced a race of moral giants. But parents also wonder about permissiveness and its effects, and just how much of it is currently in disfavor and exactly why. They have been told to love their children, and then all will be well. There isn't the slightest doubt that love is essential. Without it no child can ever learn right from wrong. The love his parents feel for him and show him constitutes his very first lesson in ethical behavior. But love alone cannot guarantee the development of a sound ethical character, and parents are now aware of that, too. Thus, with the oversimplified love-conquers-all dictum definitely on the wane, the whole question of how to teach youngsters right from wrong remains. What is more, it remains hazy.

It is precisely because parents do want their children to grow into strong, able human beings that they are concerned about this question of right and wrong. Yet on all sides—in the newspapers, in magazines, on TV, in real life—parade countless examples of adults who lie, who cheat, who steal, who loathe their neighbor. Corruption in politics, unethical business dealings, graft, and cheating are commonplace fixtures on our national scene. Even more disturbing is the apparent widespread acceptance of these practices and attitudes as a part of the American way of life.

Is honesty corny?

Being honest actually seems to carry a stigma in some quarters. This was recently brought out in the testimony of one large-city policeman who explained why he took an outside job in violation of departmental rules. He said it might sound "corny," but it gave him "a good feeling when I know I'm not on the take, that I've got an honest outside job that brings in enough to keep me honest."

Thoughtful and sensitive parents do not want to raise their children with the idea that honesty is "corny," that even a little bit of crime pays—that anything you can get away with is probably legitimate. They take seriously their responsibility for helping to shape the lives of the future members of society. They want their youngsters not only to be happy, but to be strong and courageous, willing to stand up for ideals and principles. They want them not only to feel and know the difference between right and wrong, but to be able to follow through with both words and actions. It is hardly a parental goal to raise a whole new generation who must reach for tranquilizers every time the going gets a little rough!

Guidelines, not formulas

Parents have been told that it is not only all right to set limits for their children, but that it is essential that they do so. But how, when, what? They wonder, they worry, they ask: "Will our standards automatically carry over to our children?" "How potent are outside influences?" "What about the young person from a loving family who cannot seem to distinguish between good and evil? How and why does that happen?" "Why do churchgoing youngsters get into trouble just about as often as nonchurchgoers?"

Aren't there any guidelines for right and wrong that fit

all families, even though adjustments have to be made here and there to allow for differences?

Of course there are guidelines, but there is no magical formula. It takes strength and courage to be a parent. It takes humor. It takes self-knowledge. It takes conviction. It takes the willingness to look at your own problems fearlessly and frankly. It takes the wisdom to recognize your mistakes and to learn from them. It takes the ability to roll with the punches. And it requires the realization that not *everything* unpleasant or difficult that happens is your fault. Does this sound like a superhuman job? No one would claim that successful parenthood is simple and easy, but we all know that despite everything there is no more important or rewarding or interesting job anywhere.

The myth of common sense

Right here is a good time to explore and explode the myth of common sense as the road to successful parenthood. This latest cliché is being bandied about with much frequency, but without much thought. "Just use your common sense," the prescription runs. "That's the way your grandparents managed, and they didn't do so badly." Aside from the fact that times have changed since our grandparents' day, there is plenty of reason to question that simple injunction. All we have to do is look around us. How much strength and health has common sense alone produced? How much has it contributed to the establishment of sound values? What prejudices lurk behind its comforting sound? How much ignorance can it hide? True, common sense does have an important place in child care. It is common sense to stop Mark from downing twelve banana splits. It is common sense to set a reasonable bedtime for Mary Lou. It is common sense to teach Tony to swim. But it takes more than common sense to become and to produce a reasonable, ethical human being.

This is not to suggest that it takes an "ideal" family

where there is never any friction or unhappiness, where parents never make mistakes. Such a family simply does not exist. It is literally impossible not to make mistakes, and you will make your share. But they do not have to be fatal, and they do not mean that your child will not learn right from wrong. No parent can know all his child's needs. Your child himself does not know, and could not tell you if he did. What is important is not the mistakes themselves, but how quickly you catch on to them and correct them.

Here is where knowledge and understanding can help. There is a body of scientific knowledge about children and their development that can enlighten parents and perhaps relieve them of needless worries. When a parent discovers that his youngster's odd behavior of the moment is typical for his age group, it helps. When he learns that other mothers and fathers have faced and met similar problems, that helps, too. Parents must use their own judgment, and thoughtful parents do just that when they read, discuss with others, learn and apply some of the knowledge about child rearing and family relationships that is available to them. They know that there are no simple hard-and-fast rules to follow that will prevent all mistakes or solve all difficulties for them, and they know that no one, not even the most learned experts, are as familiar with their particular child, their special situation, their family problems as they themselves are. They know, too, that while they are the most important influences in their youngsters' lives, they are not the only ones, and that things can go wrong through no fault of theirs and through circumstances that are beyond their control. But knowledge and understanding are important—and that includes knowing and understanding themselves as well as their youngsters. Knowledge and understanding bolster so-called common sense, illumine past experience, help correct mistakes, and point the way to wise guidance.

Knowledge of child development helped the Morans

over a trying period with their son Johnny. Until he entered fourth grade, Johnny Moran had been a healthy co-operative boy, obviously devoted to his parents. Then, almost overnight, they noticed quite a change. Outwardly he no longer seemed to want their approval, and he didn't make much effort to please them. Formerly loving and confiding, he now seemed to have lost his affectionate disposition. He could hardly wait to slam out of the house and join his pals, leaving his homework undone whenever he thought he could get away with it. He began to contradict practically everything, saying: "You're wrong, you don't know." Sometimes he just ignored what his mother considered a reasonable request, like washing his hands before meals, taking a bath more than just once in a while, or picking up his clothes at least some of the time. Most nights, Mrs. Moran had to call him in to dinner three times before he seemed to hear. His vocabulary came to include a couple of four-letter words which the Morans knew Johnny had not learned at home. He was obviously more intent on making a good impression on his pals than on his parents.

Now if the Morans had not learned that this was a phase most nine-year-olds go through, they might have been unduly upset, and their handling of him quite different. But they did realize that many youngsters around his age go through this stage, and that these children must do so in order to move ahead to the next step in their development. It was important to Johnny to band together with others like himself and to win their respect and loyalty. Even though Johnny's attitude was not easy to cope with, the Morans knew all this was natural, and their knowledge helped them to be understanding.

At the same time, the Morans didn't just sit back and accept everything as a passing phase. Take for instance, the matter of "dirty" language, or tough talk. Mrs. Moran didn't act shocked because she knew that most children pick up these words and experiment with them. But she did let Johnny know that she didn't particularly want to hear them. Otherwise, he might well have got the idea that anything goes at home.

On many another time she put her foot down. One was the day Johnny wanted to wear his sneakers to school in a raging snowstorm. But on the whole she gave him plenty of leeway. Neither she nor her husband ever let Johnny ride roughshod over them, but they managed to let him know that they loved him even when his behavior wasn't making a hit with them. Hard as it often was for them to believe, they were aware that Johnny needed their approval. Just as he had when he was younger, he wanted them to think he was good.

Ethical living starts early

Long before a child has reached school age, he has learned a great deal about what his parents consider "good" behavior, what sort of behavior wins their approval and makes him feel good as a person. The seeds of ethical living start to take root when a child is still very young. In subtle ways and direct ways, in the course of day-to-day family living, a child learns to value trust, honesty, kindness, justice—though he is still a long way from knowing them by these names. He is learning about them, nevertheless, as he sees his parents live out these very qualities in their relationships with him.

A child's ethical values are learned, both when he is aware of it and when he is not, from those he admires and wants to be like. If Joey loves his father and his father loves him, he will want to copy his way of doing things. If Alice loves her mother and is loved by her, she will want to be like her mother. In addition, the love and affection that parents show their child, and their enjoyment and appreciation of him as he grows, help him to feel important and worthwhile as a person while he is still very young. The warmth and acceptance that he experiences within the

23

family help him to feel that life is good, that *he* is good.

It is during these early years that a child develops trust in his immediate world of people. This trust helps him to gain confidence in himself as he grows. And confidence in himself and in others not only helps him to enjoy life, but gives him courage and will eventually show him the way to ethical behavior. The child who has been helped to develop these feelings of trust and confidence can later on become the person with enough inner strength to stand up for a cause that is just and fair, even though it may not be popular. But he has a good deal of growing and learning to do before this goal can be reached, and none of it can be rushed. Only so much can be expected of him along the way. Growth not only takes time—it is uneven. Ethical growth is no exception. His family will continue to play a major part in the development of ethical growth for a long time to come.

The fallacy of togetherness

But families don't have an easy time of it today. Economic and social changes have transformed old, established patterns of family living. They have left us without the clearly defined roles of our grandparents' day and with a vague uncertainty about where we really fit in and what we are expected to do. Perhaps this has contributed to the clamorous insistence in recent years on family togetherness. While the values and the joys of happy, close-knit family living can hardly be overestimated, the togetherness campaign is something else again—and its influence on parents bears looking into.

Much current advertising seems designed to hold up a mirror to an ideal American family living an ideal American life. Everywhere we see pictures of a young family with a small, appealing girl who looks like (and is often dressed like) the mother, and a slightly smaller boy, who in turn looks like the father. Closer inspection of these smiling young faces reveals that not only do the children look like the parents, but the parents look like the children. They are simply larger versions of their own offspring. Bigger but somehow just as downy and immature.

One sees these four charming, sun tanned and carefree youngsters planning a picnic or enjoying a barbecue, looking at TV or going to the movies, or swimming at the beach or pool. But one cannot by any stretch of an elastic imagination think of them apart, as separate and distinct individuals, going their separate ways to read a book, paint a picture, invent a gadget, write a poem—or even just to sulk. Don't these "families" whom real parents are being gently persuaded to like—and be like—and buy like—ever quarrel? Don't they ever exchange a cross word? More disturbing, doesn't any one of them ever need to be alone to think? Apparently not. The solitude demanded for creative and intellectual effort, the search for self essential to real ethical growth, these obviously just aren't in the cards for this amiable group of "look-alike" youngsters.

None of this would seem too important if it were not that some parents out of their own uncertainties have taken seriously this always-together, never-apart theme. Some have been interpreting it too literally.

To the Graysons, for example, it seemed a safe, ready-made answer to their own insecurity. They had hopped on the togetherness bandwagon early, along with others in their suburban community. The family spent practically all of its free time—self-consciously and with premeditation—doing things together. Not long ago Mrs. Grayson brought seven-year-old Janie, the youngest of three, into town to see the doctor. After the appointment she dropped the youngster off at the house of an old friend.

Aunt Kay, as she was known to the children, was a sensitive and observant woman. She had always seen Janie in the company of her sister and brother, both young teenagers. Once in a while Aunt Kay was a little concerned about Janie, who seemed at times overcompliant, oversubmissive. But on this visit, alone with Aunt Kay, Janie chattered away, vastly more assertive and self-expressive than she could ever bring herself to be when her scene-stealing siblings were around. Before it was time for her to be picked up, Aunt Kay told Janie how much she had enjoyed hearing about her school, her likes and dislikes, and the rest. Janie's reply was: "I love to go somewhere alone. It makes me feel like my own real self."

Every child needs an independent identity

What kind of self can a child develop who has no independent identity of his own? What kind of self can twelve-year-old Harold develop, for example, if he can never shut himself in his room alone, secure in the knowledge that the sign on his door, reading "Keep Out—This Means You" will be respected?

If a youngster has not all along done the kinds of breaking away from the family that enable him to come back in, stronger and wiser, with a deepening understanding of right and wrong, it can be a very meager self indeed that he develops. Too encompassing an emphasis on family togetherness can keep one from knowing and coming to terms with oneself, one's purpose and meaning. It can keep one from seeking and discovering a place and from gaining acceptance in the wider world outside. It can keep one from developing a real sense of right and wrong and the courage to live by it.

How to teach a child right from wrong involves every aspect of family life. A child who is eventually to feel what is right, in the larger sense must first feel right inside himself. He must know that he is loved and respected and accepted for himself—just as he is. He must be given reasonable discipline which will in turn lead to the development of self-discipline, an essential ingredient in ethical behavior. He must see a pattern of consistency in what his parents say about right and wrong and what they do about it. For example, a father who preaches honesty and then boasts about how he put one over on the income tax collector does serious harm to his child's ethical growth.

Love, understanding, discipline, and example are all important in teaching a child right from wrong. We shall examine these ingredients in detail as we consider various aspects of right and wrong in specific situations throughout this book.

No one special trick of training will insure the development of mature ethical conduct, but parents in their total dealings with their youngsters will find many ways to teach right from wrong. In the following chapters we will see some of these ways as we look at parents and their children under many circumstances, some trying, some pleasurable, some puzzling, some painful. We will consider outside influences, good and harmful. We will pose questions, though often there may be no specific answers. We will see why parents and children act as they do in certain instances, how their actions make others feel, what the consequences can be. In this way parents can get clues to their own behavior, for it is largely (though by no means solely) through that behavior that images of right and wrong are implanted in the minds and hearts of their children.

Chapter two

GLAD TO BE A BOY . . .

PROUD TO BE A GIRL

We have come a long way from the days when parents thought it shameful for their children to ask about sex and wrong for them to answer their youngsters' questions. Mothers and fathers may still not find it a comfortable subject to discuss, but they try not to duck it. They ask for help on how to tell, and just how much; on when to tell, and just what words to use. They know that it is more than a simple matter of giving information once or twice.

Parents cannot breathe a sigh of relief and feel that the job is all done once they have answered a child's first questions, or introduced the subject themselves if a child has not yet asked. They know that information has to be repeated over and over again in the same ways and in different ways with each step in a child's development. But helping a child to form clear, ethical standards about sex which will stand him in good stead as he grows up involves much more than straightforward and repeated explanations of where babies come from, and reasonably relaxed parental attitudes about sex, important though these are. It takes a long time and it takes more than words, for sex education covers many things.

How to foster healthy attitudes

No child can develop healthy, ethical standards about sex if he is not helped to have a healthy attitude about his own body—its functions, its products, its apertures. As a baby he begins to acquire an attitude about his body and about the bodies of others. Patterns of feeling develop from the first simple routines of his life as he is fed and bathed and lovingly cared for. He learns more as he senses how his mother and father feel about each other and about him. He learns from what they say and how they act in many situations, though probably no single everyday experience has a permanent effect. It is the total climate of feeling and behavior that counts.

The day the Gordon baby discovered his hands was almost as exciting for his parents as it was for him. There he was in his crib, lying on his back, cooing and waving his arms in the air. All of a sudden his eyes took in his hands— and gradually it began to dawn on him that they belonged to him. The fascination with which he studied them brought a smile to Ann Gordon's face and she called her husband Bill over to watch the baby's intense concentration. They knew that soon he would be aware that he could move his fingers and his hands to and fro and that he would then find his toes. Eventually on this marvelous voyage of discovery he would find other parts of his body. He would touch and handle his sex organs just as he had his toes and ears and lips. The Gordons knew that this was natural. They would take it calmly—they knew that there was nothing wrong in it. The Gordon baby was off to a good start.

Cora and Ted Jones are proud of three-year-old Teddy. He has an active, alert mind and is interested in practically everything. He took his toy truck apart the other day to find out how it was made, and what's more he was able to put it together again. His parents were certainly proud of him. But just this morning his curiosity took another turn. His mother found him in the neighbor's back yard undressing little Joan to find out how *she* was made. Nobody was proud of him this time. They scolded him severely, declaring Joan's house out of bounds for a while. Teddy may not stop his investigating, but he now has the idea that his parents feel that it is "wrong" to be curious about some things.

Twelve-year-old Hank has just heard his first talk on hygiene at school. The teacher explained to the boys about the reproductive organs, told them something about the sex act, and the mutual love and respect it betokens in marriage. But nothing at home bears out what Hank has just learned in school. Hank's father has a violent temper which he controls not at all, unleashing most of it on Hank's mother. Will Hank find it easy to believe his teacher? How much confusion about sex and violence is there likely to be in his mind as a result of what goes on at home?

Janie, just sixteen months old, was sitting in the bathroom on her potty. She had just had a bowel movement and was happily engaged in smearing it around. When her mother came in, she slapped Janie's hands and said, "That's nasty. You're a bad girl." By her tone and her words and her actions she got across to Janie her feelings about the body, its products, and its functions. And these attitudes will help form the basis for Janie's feelings of clean and dirty—or right and wrong—about the way her body works.

Parents place a high premium on curiosity—and rightly so. They say to their children, "Pat the bunny," or "Feel this nice smooth stone," or "Let's find out what makes this wheel turn." In a variety of ways they encourage their youngsters to explore, to touch, to learn. They are proud and pleased when the response is eager and enthusiastic. But they sometimes forget that young children are naturally curious about their own bodies and about each other's, too. And this curiosity does not generally meet with the same high level of parental approval. But mothers and fathers who know that such interest is natural can take it in their stride if their very young children attempt to satisfy it by looking to see how another child is made. For all children want to find out not only what others of the opposite sex look like, but also if others of the same sex look like them. And they want to know for certain.

Satisfy your child's curiosity

Even better than simply putting up with a little investigating, parents themselves can help their children learn. In families with young children of both sexes there are many natural learning opportunities: when you bathe them or get them ready for bed, for example. And for those families without such easy learning opportunities, there are ways and means of satisfying this natural curiosity. Perhaps there are young cousins or a neighbor's baby. If you bring your youngster along when you visit them, or invite them over to visit you, just being around at bath- or bedtime will give your child a chance to observe and to ask questions.

Questions are the acceptable substitutes for direct exploration. A child's initial impulse is to explore exactly as a puppy does, by looking, touching, tasting, sniffing. But these ways of satisfying curiosity are not permitted—nor can they be. And here is where the freedom to speak and ask is of vital importance. Knowing the right names for body parts and functions and using them appropriately in ordinary conversation helps bring questions out into the

31

open. In the course of satisfying your child's curiosity by allowing him freedom to ask and learn, you must also set up barriers at each stage in his development.

This takes great skill and no one is perfect at it, but you can let your child know what is not permitted without giving him the idea that he is bad, or that his body and his feelings get him into trouble. For example, if you discover your young child in sex play with others (and practically all children try this), you help him best not by shaming or scolding him, but by being firm and matter-of-fact. A clear-cut, but not angry, "I don't want you to do that any more" helps get your point across without making him feel overwhelmingly guilty and ashamed.

Masturbation, too, often worries parents. Those who are not overly troubled about it in an infant sometimes wonder if they should do something when they notice it later, say at three or four. It is safe to say, just as it was earlier, that masturbation is normal. If you can consider it a natural part of the growing-up process, you can keep your child from feeling too guilty and fearful about it. You can accomplish this best by taking it calmly and letting him know, if he seems worried about it, that it is something most youngsters try. He probably feels some anxiety about it, anyway, no matter what your attitude. Your job is not to ignore it, but to let him know that all youngsters want to do it, that most of them do, and that they can usually stop when they try.

A youngster who masturbates a great deal—enough to interfere with his regular interests and play activities—is a child who has other problems. Something is amiss in such a child's life, and it is important for parents to find out the cause. They may need professional help to do so. But if a child has plenty of interests and playmates, if he seems happy and unworried, then there is no need for concern.

Very young boys and girls may worry about the difference in how they are made and whether it was meant to be that way. A little girl may wonder if she, too, once had a penis. "Where did mine go." she may ask. Or a little boy may say, "Will someone take mine away?" Setting children straight is important not only for now, but for later. Telling a little girl that that's the way she was meant to be made and that that's how her mother is made, and moreover that that's how you *like* her to be made, is just what she needs to hear. And, of course, a boy has to know that his penis will not be taken away, that he, too, was meant to be made the way he is, and that it is not going to change.

Help your child ask

Some children may never ask these questions or any others about sex. Sensing that you might not be pleased if he did, the child does not want to risk courting your disapproval. It is up to you to give the cue. Referring naturally to these things gives a child permission to acknowledge and express his curiosity. If, for example, you mention that a neighbor or a friend is going to have a baby, then your child knows that this whole subject is one that can be talked about—that you talk about it, that he can, too.

A few parents say they are reluctant to satisfy a child's curiosity because it may sharpen his interest or make him immodest or give him false notions of right and wrong behavior. This is simply not so. Remaining silent about a subject does not mean that it will go away or that a youngster is no longer curious. A child can sense a parent's discomfort or disapproval, and he may bury his feelings at the time only to have them erupt in one disabling form or another later on.

Help a child value himself

Does it sound farfetched to make this connection between a child's bodily curiosity and his eventual development of a sense of right and wrong? There is a real and an important link. When you begin early to help a child to accept himself, to be "glad to be a boy" and "proud to be a girl," you are laying the foundation for future relationships and standards. For in helping a child to like and value himself, you are preparing him also to like and value another. A healthy acceptance of his own body is essential if he is to develop ethical sex attitudes as he grows up.

It is hard for a boy to be "glad to be a boy" or a girl to feel "proud to be a girl" if parents do not value their youngsters for what they are. Little Robby was the Murray's fourth child, a fourth boy! After their initial disappointment, they agreed that it was foolish to have counted on a girl, and of course they loved Robby. But without even knowing she was doing it, Robby's mother treated him quite differently than she had the older boys. She dressed him in clothes that were a little too fussy, could not bear to cut his curls, and tended to overprotect him in many ways, large and small. Wanting, as all youngsters do, to please his mother, Robby learned quickly the value of shunning the rough-and-tumble ways of the other boys.

June Curtis was frankly a disappointment to her father who had looked forward eagerly to having a son. He was even more disappointed when the doctor told him that there could be no more children. So Mr. Curtis proceeded to act as though June were the boy he had always wanted. He nicknamed her Jay, and as she grew older he encouraged her to climb higher, run faster, play ball more strenuously than she was naturally inclined to do. He was proud when she could beat the boys at their own games. It was not difficult for June to discover that the more she acted like a boy, the more she pleased her father.

Accept your child for what he is

It is a good idea to look carefully at these examples of really well-meaning parents. They did not neglect their children. Actually, they spent a good deal of time with them. But one thing stands out clearly: If you want a child to accept himself happily as he is, you must do so, too. And he must feel that you do, wholeheartedly.

Often without meaning to, parents devalue the sex of their children and make them wish that they were something they are not and cannot be. Occasionally children all on their own begin to devalue themselves. Sometimes it can happen when a little boy envies a younger sister, or a little girl envies her younger or older brother. But if parents are quick to notice it, they can keep it from developing into something serious. They must try to discover why their youngster thinks the grass looks greener on the other side of the fence. Then they can make positive efforts to counteract this impression by giving him many chances to find out that it is not so, and to build up his pride in his own sex. Perhaps a father could arrange to spend more time with his son, or a mother do something very special with her daughter. Mothers and fathers will want to provide many opportunities for daughters to be "proud to be girls" and sons "glad to be boys."

Then there are some parents who have very firm notions of what boys should be like and what girls should be like. In their determination to make their boys he-men and their girls models of femininity, they lose track of the fact that there is plenty of leeway in these matters of maleness and femaleness. A four-year-old boy who likes to play with a doll is not destined to turn into a sissy. Nor will a ten-year-old who finds it fun to try his hand at cooking now and then. And there does not have to be anything unfemale about a girl's interest in carpentry or chemistry sets. A too rigid insistence on patterns perhaps once considered male or female fits neither today's world nor the children in it. Boys will be helped to grow to manliness and girls to womanliness by their own acceptance of themselves as they are and by the examples they see at home of their own mothers and fathers, not by any words or trappings or pre-conceived notions of what is masculine and what is feminine.

Feelings speak louder than words

For the most part, mothers and fathers today try to answer their children's questions, telling them what they want to know—neither too much nor too little—but what they can take in at each stage of their development. Many good books and films are available that not only provide a background of factual material but also help parents take a look at their own feelings and attitudes about sex, what they consider right and wrong behavior, and why. For it is really their feelings that they are getting across to their children, no matter how accurate their words.

Not only actions, but feelings speak louder than anything you have to say. It is important, then, to examine them carefully. Maybe some are not clear to you, maybe some cannot or should not be changed, but trying to understand your feelings will help to make you more responsive to your youngsters' needs and more sensitive in your efforts to guide them. Talking things out with other parents often helps to clarify feelings. Arranging through parents' groups for a film, a talk, a panel discussion are some of the ways parents become free to take a deeper look at their own feelings and how they came to be.

The Roberts family was doing just such a conscientious job, but they were brought up short one morning when they picked up the newspaper to find an account of an unsavory sex scrape a fourteen-year-old youngster in a neighboring town had got himself into. Tom Roberts voiced some of his doubts, "You know, Mary, I'm worried. Maybe we're giving these youngsters too much information."

"Maybe we're not doing it right," his wife answered.

They were both alarmed—this episode had hit pretty close to home. Tom wondered if perhaps they ought to stop answering questions so freely, and Mary speculated on whether they had done a good enough job. But as they talked about it, things began to clear up. They really did not have the vaguest idea about the background of this unknown youngster, but they did know their own Teddy. They knew, too, that youngsters do not get into such serious trouble suddenly and with no warning at all. The Robertses felt certain that their total relationship with their son was good. Teddy knew how they felt about right and wrong and how he felt. Mr. and Mrs. Roberts were sorry for the boy whose story was spread all over the newspaper, and for his parents, but they knew he did not get into trouble just because he had been given sex information. There was more to it than that.

As a matter of fact, more needs to be known and understood about this whole problem of helping youngsters to develop sound sex attitudes and clear, ethical standards. Many problems exist to which no easy answers can be given. On the whole, parents have tried to do a good job, and have succeeded reasonably well with their young children, but not well enough to make any of us complacent. It becomes even harder when these same youngsters reach adolescence.

When adolescent problems arise . . .

Most teen-agers go through a period when they cannot confide fully in their parents. Because they have such mixed feelings about their mothers and fathers, direct talk about sexual matters is almost impossible for many of them. This lack of communication disturbs many conscientious parents who feel that all their efforts at keeping the communications lines open have now failed. The lines have not been torn down—they may be temporarily out of order, but your messages still get through. And so do others—from friends, friends' parents, teachers, physicians, clergymen, other adults. Talking about sex disturbs many parents now that these youngsters have reached physiological maturity and the whole subject is no longer in the realm of theory. It was one thing to tell four-year-olds where babies come from, but quite another to talk with teen-agers who have strong sexual impulses of their own.

Parents of teen-agers often ask: Is it wrong for these youngsters to go steady? Should we look the other way at kissing and petting? How can we be sure they will not experiment further?

. . . take stock of your own feelings

To get even a clue as to how to respond and to know how to set up the necessary barriers, parents must again take a good look at their own beliefs and feelings. When you know what you feel and believe in and communicate it to your youngster, you are helping him form clear, ethical standards for himself. It helps to remember that you yourself probably struggled with many of the same feelings he has, worried about the same problems, when you were younger. It will help your youngster to know that you did. You will want to tell him so. Bringing your own mistakes out into the open, and talking about their consequences, can be a valuable learning experience for your adolescent.

The going-steady problem had become almost the number-one topic of discussion in the Levin household. Practically everybody in her crowd went steady, sixteen-year-old Margie told her parents. They knew she was telling the truth, but they were not so sure they approved. Equally, they were not so sure that they wanted Margie to feel different and out of things. But that did not help Margie much right at the moment because she had to tell Jerry by Saturday night whether she could be his steady.

So the Levins temporized—they told Margie she could go steady with Jerry, but for no more than three months. She was not the least bit unhappy to hear this, and to their amazement, only two months later Margie was going steady with a different boy. So were most of the others in her crowd.

To Mr. and Mrs. Levin, going steady had a frightening sound of permanency about it. Despite the evidence to the contrary in their community, they still worried that it might mean what it had in their youth—exclusive dating leading to marriage. But to Margie and her friends it meant one at a time, not one for always. And for those youngsters the custom had real value. Many of them were awkward and confused in their first attempts to go out together, and developing social ease with each other was difficult. Their first steady dates were generally with another couple who were also going steady. After all, when there were four of them, somebody was bound to think of something to say. Young people need practice in learning how to get along with each other if they are to be able to form mature relationships later on.

Not all going-steady problems are as uncomplicated as Margie's. Some youngsters her age become more serious about each other, and for longer periods of time. Parents will have to summon up all their patience and understanding if this happens and call on their youngsters to do so, too. Together they can discuss why it is important to learn to know a number of boys and girls. Only by meeting a variety of people and learning about different temperaments and values and interests can teen-agers begin to choose wisely. They themselves know that they do not have enough experience or judgment yet to pick a permanent partner.

Be calm and show confidence

When you take the dating relationships of your young people calmly, they are more likely to listen to you, for these sixteen-year-olds are not so sure of themselves in these situations as they sometimes pretend to be. And, of course, you will resist any temptation to laugh at them or tease them. Their feelings deserve consideration. They are working hard at the serious business of learning to form real relationships.

Having made your feelings and judgments clear, you will try to avoid questioning adolescents about every single detail of their dates. Naturally, you have a right to know where and with whom your youngsters are spending their time because those things are important, but nagging or open disapproval creates nothing but resentment. They will sense your disapproval even if it is unspoken and resent the fact that you did not voice it. Teenagers generally respond well when their parents have confidence in them, although they understandably do not like too much cross-examination about nonessential details. It takes all the joy and mystery out of life.

But kissing and petting cannot be called nonessential details. How do parents handle this problem? Not like Mrs. Ellis, we hope. She put her foot down and told Wendy that even a good-night kiss was forbidden under any and all circumstances. Since this practice was indulged in by practically all the youngsters Wendy knew, and since most of the parents were aware of it, Mrs. Ellis really had put herself in an untenable position. She certainly could not police everyone, and her attitude was not much help to Wendy. Her fear made her clamp down so tightly on Wendy that any chance of closeness between them, any talking out the whole problem of kissing and petting and explaining why barriers have to be set up, was impossible.

Like most mothers and fathers, Mrs. Ellis was worried about how far the kissing and petting would go. Would it stop right there? Parents, aware of the explosive nature of the situation, realize that it can be but a short step to further intimacy. This is not always so obvious to young people. Parents must help them understand the potential dangers, not by clamping down on simple physical expressions of affection or by shutting their eyes to what is going on around them, but by maintaining the kind of attitude where free discussion can take place. The real problem is not to try to ban the kissing, which is probably universal, but to prepare a girl or boy to handle it.

A youngster may say that he can handle these situations and not let them get out of control, but he cannot yet foresee what they may lead to. Parents can. Aware that you are on his side, your child can accept your firmness and your counsel. It is up to you to share your convictions with him and discuss them openly. Your teen-agers are entitled to know what you think and to be part of the total planning for their welfare. You are probably not going to win a popularity contest with them right now, and you should not try to. You will help them best to know right from wrong if you are firm when you need to be, explain why, and stick by it.

You no doubt believe that sexual intercourse should not take place until marriage, and you have told your young-sters so. And because you have been open and honest with them, they believe you. You have helped them have a healthy, comfortable attitude about sex and its significance in human relations. They know that it is part of love, an expression of very deep feeling for another person, and that it achieves its fullest satisfaction in an enduring, mature partnership. You have discussed with them the reasons for control at their age and explained that biological readiness is not enough. They can understand and accept your guidance, and are usually grateful for it to bolster up their own sometimes shaky self-control.

Right and wrong in sex relationships, as in everything else, are rooted in true self-discipline. If all along in your total dealings with your children, you have helped them to feel reasonably good about themselves, if you have guided them on their way to becoming mature, responsible adults, then you have also given them the capacity to defer gratification. You have helped them to develop the ability to wait until they are fully ready.

No youngster in his mid-teens is emotionally prepared for something so complex as sexual experience. And usually in those cases where it does occur, it is almost certain evidence that something has gone very wrong somewhere along the line.

Sexual experiences in the mid-teens may represent a misguided search for love, an expression of hostility toward parents, a rivalry with contemporaries. They may be a manifestation of doubts about a teen-ager's own attractiveness to the opposite sex. A boy may wonder about his competence as a young man, and the need to "prove" himself may lead him into premature sexual activities. Some girls with inner doubts about their ability to attract boys may feel that the one sure way to gain acceptance is to engage in sexual activities. The more self-confidence you have helped your youngsters to develop and the surer they feel about themselves as they are, the easier it is for them to wait for the right time and the right person.

Speak out on sex relationships

One of the marks of growing maturity and of all ethical behavior is the ability to delay or postpone gratification—not indefinitely, but for a time. Premature sexual experience is usually evidence of conflict and unhappiness. And the sexual activity itself leads only to further conflict and unhappiness. Therefore, parents need to take a firm stand to help prevent their sons and daughters from entering into premature sexual relations.

Often these young people need reassurance that their sex feelings are normal, desirable, and healthy, and that all teen-agers experience them. If they know that other adolescents also have strong sex urges along with a great drive to masturbate, their anxieties about their own sexual interest and any compulsive element in it will lessen. It is important for parents to recognize that teen-agers want very much to grow up, to fall in love, to silence their doubts about their own sexual adequacy. But it is equally important for parents to point out the responsibilities involved, the need for control, the unreadiness in the total sense at this age, and the dangers of giving way to impulse.

The capacity for love

From the very beginning, as you help your son to be "glad to be a boy" and your daughter "proud to be a girl," you are teaching them right from wrong. Only if a human being has a healthy acceptance of his own body can he have a healthy and ethical attitude about sex. You convey this all-important self-acceptance to your children as you speak openly and frankly, satisfy their curiosity, acknowledge their feelings and their right to them, and treat body functions as normal and human, not as disgusting and dirty. You give them freedom to grow and become independent, but you also impose reasonable and sensible limits. Respecting your youngsters, you help them respect themselves and others. Loving them, you give them the capacity for love.

Chapter three

SPARE THE CHILD

"How can I teach Andy to mind without being too tough on him?" "Won't being strict with Mary Ellen make her neurotic?" "What's wrong with spanking my ten-year-old when he constantly disobeys?" "Isn't it harmful to frustrate Susie—she's only six?"

What permissiveness is all about

Parents ask questions like these over and over again. They want to know how to teach their children right from wrong without either clamping down too much or being too free and easy. Most agree on the why of discipline—the how of it is another matter. Some parents have been confused about the concept of permissiveness. A few have misconstrued it to mean that you permit a child to do whatever he wants—that you never thwart him, that you allow him to "express" himself all the time. This came about largely through an early misapplication to child rearing of a principle that is sometimes a necessary temporary stratagem in psychotherapy.

Actually, rightly used, permissiveness, or "permissive discipline," is simply a more intelligent approach than the old method of "spare the rod and spoil the child." Years ago it was generally assumed that children were born "bad" and therefore had to be forced to learn to behave—had, in fact, to be trained rigorously, even beaten or deprived, to mold them into respectable human beings. Children were taught early in life to obey their parents' commands unquestioningly. Then, as more and more was learned about children—how they grow and develop and learn—this rigid, tyrannical type of upbringing gave way to a more reasonable, relaxed, and friendly approach to child care.

Today's parents are aware that children are not born "bad," that, if anything, they prefer to be good—at first, because they want and need their parents' love and approval. They come to identify that love and approval with what is right and good. Only much later on in their development will children be able to make the distinction between winning parental approval and their own concept of goodness.

When you begin to set limits for your child that are

45

appropriate for his stage of development, not unreasonably restrictive, but ones he can understand and accept comfortably, you are giving him his first practical lessons in right and wrong. As he grows in his ability to impose reasonable limits on himself, your discipline of him gradually gives way to self-discipline. You cannot expect self-discipline to emerge at all until your child is about five, and it will not become a stable part of his personality until he is twice that age. Only at the end of adolescence will he be ready to take over the controls himself.

While a child's desire to be loved is an essential ingredient in his ethical growth, love alone, as we have pointed out earlier, will not guarantee the development of a sound, ethical character. Giving love without imposing limits encourages a child to demand love without fulfilling any of its obligations. Imposing limits without giving love fosters only rebellion and a rejection of all self-discipline. Most parents understand that it is not love to allow a child to do whatever he pleases. They know that children learn the difference between what they should and should not do only in a climate of warm acceptance and friendly firmness.

Feeling "bad" is normal

This climate of warm acceptance must include accepting a child's feelings and his right to have them. While we know that all children want to *be* good, we also know that they very often *feel* bad. In other words, there are times when they feel angry, destructive, envious, hateful. Perhaps the single most important contribution parents can make to their children's ethical development is to let them know that their "bad" feelings are normal and that all other children have them, too. This does not mean granting them the right to inflict those feelings on others. It does mean giving them the freedom to acknowledge them, to talk about them openly—without shame and without guilt.

When a child understands that it is permissible to feel anger toward his parents, his brothers and sisters, that very knowledge helps him get over the anger. More important, it keeps him from feeling overwhelmingly guilty because of it. The child who is always "good," who never talks back, who is superconscientious, may be afraid of losing his parents' love if he lets his feelings show.

A mother gives her child vital reassurance when she can say, "I understand—you wish the baby (or Daddy) weren't here so I could spend all my time with you. Every child feels that way sometimes. Daddy did and I did when we were little. But my parents loved me even when I felt that way, and we love you, too, no matter what you feel." When parents make opportunities to discuss a child's feelings with him right out in the open, to let him talk about them freely, then the child knows that he *and* his feelings are accepted—and acceptable. He need not bury them deep down out of conscious awareness where they may remain to plague him in one form or another for the rest of his life.

Expressing feelings constructively

Let us go back and examine the difference between encouraging a child to express his feelings in words, but not in destructive actions. Many parents are not clear about this distinction: *it is very important*. To give a child free rein to act out his anger will do him harm and increase his guilt and shame, not lessen them. His fear of your disapproval and his desire for your love will prevent him from translating most of his angry feelings into actions. If he does overstep, he needs to know that this is something you do not allow. Losing control completely can terrify a child. It is up to you to apply the brakes *for* him.

Most parents know that children need reasonable limits, along with firm but patient guidance, and that unlimited permissiveness can be as disastrous as rigid control. Parents do best (and so do their children) when they can steer a course between overpermissiveness and overstrictness. Too rigid control ("overstrictness") hampers a child's development with a maze of dictatorial regulations and penalties that not only make him miserable but also make him unable to think for himself or to learn to take responsibility. Too little control ("overpermissiveness") expects too much of a child while not giving him enough guidance, demands decisions that he is not ready for, and fails to protect him from acts (and their consequences) which are more than he can handle.

You want your child to learn to think and act independently, but at the same time to know that he cannot behave exactly as he pleases without regard for others. This is what discipline is all about—a discipline that, as already noted, must eventually become self-discipline. It involves the ability to defer gratification for a time, to postpone pleasure when it is necessary to do so or when it interferes with the needs of someone else, or even to renounce gratification altogether in some instances. Before your child can learn right from wrong he must develop this ability to wait.

Acquiring the ability to wait

You make one small but important beginning toward this goal when your child is still an infant by using a flexible feeding schedule and planning to adjust your baby's needs to the pattern of family living. Today's mothers know that a helpless new baby needs gentle and affectionate care just as much as he needs to be kept clean and well-nourished. They know that they are not spoiling a baby by cuddling and holding him and answering his needs promptly. The old-time rigid scheduling which forced infants to cry it out until the clock said it was time to be fed is practically unheard of and certainly unheeded in this generation. Although this practice has been discarded, it is also understood that some regularity is essential as a baby grows out

48

of infancy. Well before the end of the first year, a baby can learn to wait a few minutes to be fed or changed.

He anticipates that his needs will be met—because they *have* been met in the past—and at the same time he comes to expect a certain order to life within his immediate world. He begins to develop a healthy confidence in you. He knows you will be there, and gradually he can wait for longer intervals without being uncomfortable or feeling put upon or deserted. This is the first discipline. You do not ignore his cries—but you no longer have to drop everything and fly to him the very moment he lets out a peep.

At other times he may begin to fret, not just to be fed or changed, but for your companionship, as well. This is another real need—one that you meet and like to meet. After all, it is fun to play with your baby, fun for you and for him! Later on you may not answer his call on the double every time, but if you have regularly given him his share of loving attention and companionship, you have made it possible for him to wait when he has to, to play alone happily for increasing periods of time. In this way you help your baby to have faith in you and in life, and you nurture the seeds of a loving, co-operative (in short, potentially ethical) personality.

When your baby begins to crawl and then to toddle, some discipline is again required to keep him safe, while still allowing him the freedom he needs to exercise both his mind and his muscles. Healthy curiosity spurs him to learn by touching and grabbing and tasting everything in sight.

In the Evans' household this curiosity proved to be a problem. Mrs. Evans thought she could teach sixteen-month-old Robin not to touch forbidden objects by repeatedly slapping her hands and saying, "No-no." What was the result? Robin cried, but was still determined to go after what she wanted. This into-everything stage is perfectly natural. Without exploring, how could Robin learn anything about the world around her? Wisely, Mrs. Evans decided to change her tactics and spare her baby frustration and unhappiness by simply putting away valuable objects and substituting others which Robin could investigate. True, babies of Robin's age can and do begin to learn the meaning of "No." But they learn more readily, and with a greater sense of their own worth, when the word is used sparingly.

This fair and flexible approach to discipline—based on a child's age, needs, and level of understanding—does not block his every move with restrictions and disapproval. A child who, from an early age, is appreciated and accepted for himself is less likely to balk stubbornly at restrictions necessary for his safety and for the convenience of other members of the household.

When in doubt, examine your aims

Almost every family has disciplinary problems at different ages and stages. And since each child is an individual —with his own strengths and weaknesses, his own feelings, his particular place in the family—what is best for one child may not be good for another. Besides being attuned to each child's needs, your general knowledge of how children grow and develop will help you set reasonable and appropriate standards. In addition to knowing what your children can be expected to learn, you need to know why and what you are trying to teach. When you are doubtful about a particular situation involving discipline, you might call a halt and ask yourself: What am I trying to teach? Is it important? What do my children seem to be learning?

Mrs. Williams did just those things when she found herself repeatedly reminding her seven- and nine-year-old boys to pick up after themselves, but to no avail. Seven-year-old Allen always left his clothes in a heap and his toys all over his room. His brother invariably left the family room in a mess when he and his friends played indoors.

"I've told you a hundred times—" Mrs. Williams found herself saying. Then she thought: What am I trying to teach them? Habits of neatness and respect for others, and some sense of orderliness, of course. But what did the boys seem to be learning? Not much, except that Mother kept after them constantly. Mrs. Williams began to wonder if she were not more concerned that a friend or a neighbor might drop in and find a messy house—and think her a sloppy housekeeper—than she was about her boys' habits. Were her standards too high, perhaps?

The boys obviously had a lot of energy to burn and a lot on their minds—new friends, school and schoolwork, all sorts of new things to do and see. They had trouble remembering to keep things tidy, and tidiness, after all, did not interest them very much.

Mrs. Williams decided to talk it out quietly with her sons one day and set up a few rules. She told them that they could have all the fun they wanted to in the family room and, of course, in theirs, if on Saturday mornings they each spent at least an hour, if necessary, straightening up properly. She also provided a footstool for Allen so that he could more easily hang up his clothes. She saw that it had taken a little extra effort for him to reach the hooks and the hangers. Mrs. Williams still needed to remind the boys occasionally, but not repeatedly. She expected their co-operation and got it most of the time. She wondered why it had taken her so long to realize that neatness does not come ready-made at ages seven and nine, and she speculated, too, on how many other parents expect children to learn under circumstances which make learning difficult.

Four-year-old Kenneth Parker got the idea that he was pretty bad because his mother always told him so when he displeased her. The day he crayoned all over the brand new dining room wallpaper was no exception. He was promptly spanked and labeled a "bad boy." But this punishment and name-calling taught him nothing except to feel that he really *was* a fairly undesirable character, that his mother could not possibly love him, that indeed no one good could love him.

Constantly shaming a child cannot help but make him feel unworthy. It gives him the impression that you disapprove of him totally, not of his behavior at the moment. You do not want a child ever to feel that he has lost your love because of something he has done. That is too much for him to take. But when you are angry at some misbehavior, the distinction is not always easy to make. After all, the child and his behavior are not unrelated. When you rightfully criticize the misdeed, some of your criticism is bound to spill over on the child as well. This is inevitable, and if it is appropriate to the "crime," it may well serve to avoid a repetition.

In Kenneth's case, he can be helped to learn what is accepted and what is not without being labeled "bad" or threatened with the loss of his mother's love. Of course, his mother did not stop loving him because he had spoiled her freshly papered wall, but Kenneth could not be entirely certain. She can help him understand, not by shaming him or saying she won't love him any more, but by voicing her disapproval firmly and calmly, and by considering the incident closed once she has made her point. After that, she can explain that walls are not for crayoning and give Kenneth his own paper or a blackboard to draw on. Of course, he may have to be told more than once! And she would do well to put the crayons away after he has used them where he should—so that he will not be tempted to test her out again by using them where he should not.

Anticipating a child's actions

Much of what is termed discipline involves anticipating a child's actions, demonstrating the "way we do things," providing the "we" as his bridge to full membership in the family. This is the way to be like *us* is what you are telling him—a goal he is intent on achieving. It also means providing the wherewithal and the space for constructive and creative activities. This approach eliminates the constant commands—"Don't do this," "Don't do that," "That's wrong, you are bad"—which imply that a child is an inferior, second-rate being. An occasional *don't* is necessary, but if it is occasional, it is more likely to be heard and heeded.

Does this mean you never raise your voice, never show your irritation, never get angry? Of course not. A few parents mistakenly try to conceal their feelings, but parents are people, not saints, and, anyway, feelings show through to youngsters. Mothers and fathers do get angry sometimes and shout and scold. The day Tony, aged eight, spilled red paint all over the kitchen floor, Mrs. Maxwell really exploded—but when she calmed down, she apologized to Tony for her outburst. It was only an accident. The value of her courteous, honest admission of error was not lost on him. It helped him learn that parents also make mistakes, get angry, but get over it, apologize, and let bygones be bygones.

Keep the voice down

Composure and calm are not always possible, or even desirable, but the habit of yelling at children for minor everyday irritations creates a frantic, disturbed atmosphere from which everybody wants to escape. All children (adults, too) have a way of turning deaf ears and closed minds to habitual shouting or continual nagging. If youngsters do listen, they begin to feel that they cannot ever please their parents, so why try? Or they conclude that they cannot do anything right, and this certainly eats away at self-confidence. Parents who shout at a child all the time are often themselves products of unhappy childhood experiences that deprived them of self-confidence. In turn, they may have no confidence either in their children or in their ways of disciplining them. Without even knowing it, these parents expect their children to behave badly and cannot stop them. Actually, they invite the bad behavior, and they shout not so much to discipline their children as to vent their own frustration. These parents would do well to seek professional guidance for themselves and their children.

Your firmness must be friendly

Discipline often means interfering with a child's wishes —for the child's own good. But a child cannot be expected to know this. To him it may look like malice, especially if enforced with anger. That is why your firmness must also be friendly.

Six-year-old Martha Roth wants to stay up until nine or ten o'clock at night, watching television or reading or having fun with the rest of the family. But her parents know that she needs to go to bed earlier, so they set a definite bedtime, and usually stick to it, except for special occasions. Martha's brother, Eddie, who is ten years old, likes to read in bed, but there's a curfew. Lights out at 9:30. The Roths are definite and firm most of the time, lenient occasionally. And, in general, this is a good guideline to keep in mind: Be consistent about what you expect most of the time, but not rigid and inflexible.

Reasonable regulations help your child know what is expected of him and to understand that he cannot *always* have his own way. Even though he is bound to put up a fuss at times, underneath it all he feels secure because he senses that you care enough about him to be firm. This important combination of firmness, sternness, and loving-ness is not easy for any parent to achieve. You will not always be able to manage it ideally, but you do not need to worry about the specific details of what to do and say. The feeling behind your words and actions is what counts.

Unlike the Roths, eight-year-old Howard Murphy's parents are of the old authoritarian school. Howard is not allowed to make much noise at home. He has to go easy on the roughhousing, both indoors and out. The lawn is sacred territory, and he is expected to have the utmost respect for his family's property. Howard usually submits to his parents' uncompromising demands. He is obedient, quiet, mannerly —at home. Outwardly, Howard seems submissive. Inwardly he is seething with rebellion. Only when he visits his friends does he take the opportunity to blow off steam, which in his case, is akin to blowing the lid off the pressure cooker. An outsider can readily see that Howard's parents need to relax their stern controls. In the name of discipline they are curtailing his freedom, restricting his rights as a person, and not preparing him to take over any reasonable control himself.

The Clark family, though, goes too far in another direction. They have no clear-cut rules and restrictions, and they are inclined to be inconsistent. Sometimes six-year-old Sarah is encouraged to bring her friends home, roughhousing and racing upstairs and down, having a great time. On other days Mrs. Clark shoves them all out of the house without any explanation. Sometimes Sarah climbs all over the living room furniture and nobody cares. Other times she is jumped on for the same stunt.

The Clarks have no rules about what to do where. Sometimes it is all right to cut out paper dolls in the dining room or to play with modeling clay on the coffee table. Other days, Sarah is told to play in her room and then made to clean up after herself. Mrs. Clark also has a habit of threatening Sarah: "If you go out and get your clean dress dirty, I won't let you play with the kids for a week." "No more ice pops if you don't go to bed tonight right after your TV program." But Mrs. Clark almost always forgets these threats, and Sarah really does not expect most of them to be carried out. As a result of consistent inconsistency,

Sarah is always confused about what she can and cannot do. She has to make decisions for herself which she feels uncertain about.

Relieve your child of decisions too hard for him

One of the reasons for establishing reasonable limits, and for sticking by them, is to relieve a child of decisions and responsibilities which he may not be ready to make and take. He feels on firmer ground when he is certain of a few boundaries. Even when he protests, he needs to know what time he is expected to come in for dinner, how long he can stay at his friend's house, how far from home he is allowed to go without his parents' permission.

"My mother won't let me go to the Blue Jay Supermarket," says seven-year-old Ralph. "It's too far."

"I have to go home at five-thirty," announces eight-year-old Mary, when she visits her girl friend.

"I am not allowed to eat candy before supper," says six-year-old Peggy.

It is just such simple, but explicit, ground rules that help children feel secure.

But, rules or not, no parent can *always* do everything just the way it "should be done" (even if one were totally sure what that was), and you are not *always* going to be consistent with your children. Some parents are controlling and domineering. Some are impulsive and vociferous. Others are quiet and reserved. All these differences have a bearing on the way they discipline their children. Parents cannot change overnight, but they can help their children best when they make honest efforts to understand themselves better, and when necessary, modify how and what they say and do. Too many parents insist, for example, that children say "please" to them, yet never say "please" to a child. Not enough parents recognize that even when the words they use are right, the melody may be wrong.

Children hear the discordant tune even when they shut out the words.

Just as sets of parents differ, so do individual husbands and wives. One may be more or less easygoing than the other. In your own household, for example, you may not always see eye to eye on how to manage your children. But it is important for you to talk out your attitudes together and make it a point to agree, for the most part, on what is and is not permitted. Otherwise, you may unwittingly confuse the children. This makes it difficult for them to know what to do, not because anybody's authority is undermined, but because the child cannot then go along with one parent's request without feeling disloyal to the other.

Democracy begins at home

Parents do well when their discipline is a combination of encouragement and control. Superior knowledge and accumulated experience put them in the driver's seat, in a position of authority—and rightly so. Their job is to guide, instruct, regulate, while throwing their parental weight around as little as possible. They are, and must be, "in charge," but there is a difference between being an authority and being a tyrant. And, within the family, just as in society, there is a vast difference between democracy and anarchy.

In a democratic home environment, even small children have small (not necessarily quiet) voices. They are expected to be seen and heard and listened to without being given free rein to run wild. Their feelings, needs, wishes, hopes, are taken into account. They do not necessarily come first and foremost. A child is allowed freedom to develop initiative and individuality while learning to respect the needs and wishes of others. His mistakes are not treated as crimes that must be punished, but as opportunities for learning, and he is given the freedom to learn. He is helped to feel bigger than his mistakes.

Brian Cooper had been told many times to put his bicycle in the garage at night instead of leaving it on the front lawn. He invariably "forgot" or neglected to do so. One morning when he went out to ride his bike, it was missing. Someone had stolen it. His parents knew that the loss of the bike was punishment in itself, and they did not jump on him with repeated I-told-you-so's. Brian knew that he could not have another bike for a long time. Meanwhile he had learned from a mistake. When he finally did get another bike, he did not have to be told to put it away at night. This was a hard—and somewhat expensive— lesson, but the Coopers knew that further punishment was uncalled for.

Punishment good and bad

What about punishment? Is it ever necessary? Most people think that it is, although thoughtful and sensitive parents try to keep punishment to a minimum. They try to avoid the necessity for it. By punishment, we are not talking about laying heavy hands on a child. There is no question but that this is damaging and inexcusable.

Consider Paul Spence, for example. He regularly hits his twelve-year-old boy, David, when he disobeys because he says it is the only way to make Dave toe the line. But it obviously does not work because it makes Dave sullen and resentful, and he goes right on doing things he knows he will be hit for. In resorting to such cruelty, Mr. Spence is really serving his own needs. Ashamed of what people think of him as a parent because of Dave's behavior, he is intent on showing the world that even if his child is bad, he, the father, is good. "Look," he is saying in effect, "I even beat my son when he disobeys. I am the good one."

It is probably a rare parent who has never resorted to a whack, usually in a moment of extreme annoyance. Mrs.

Jacobs does not believe in physical punishment as a method of disciplining her children. Occasionally she has resorted to a fast smack, which her youngsters understand as a quick reaction to being provoked, and nothing more. But on the whole, the atmosphere in their household is courteous and considerate, and the children absorb these attitudes from the day-to-day examples of their parents' behavior toward them and each other.

Mrs. Jacobs does find it necessary to impose penalties if and when her children repeatedly ignore or neglect what is expected of them. For example, ten-year-old Stephen is supposed to come into the house and get started on his homework at about five in the afternoon. When he repeatedly "forgot" and stayed outdoors riding his bike, Mrs. Jacobs decided not to let him use it for a few days. And when, despite reminders, eight-year-old Debbie kept going off to her friend's house, neglecting to tell her mother where she was going, and not coming home until after dinner, her mother curtailing her visiting privileges for a while. A few such deprivations, given with advance warning, are all that are needed in the Jacobs' household to help the children learn what is expected of them.

Punishment, if used at all, should be geared to a child's age and level of understanding. It is worthless—more than that, it is harmful—if a child does not understand *why* he is being punished. He must see it as a reasonable consequence of his misbehavior. Postponing punishment "until your father comes home" or "until we decide what to do" keeps a child walking around under sentence of doom! If a child feels that his parents are on his side, not always against him, he can accept punishment when it is necessary, even though it makes him angry at the time.

The best test of the efficacy of a given punishment is whether it accomplishes what you intended it to without having any harmful effects. If it makes a child misbehave more, rather than less, it has obviously missed the mark. If it makes him acutely miserable, it may be too severe. Your children will not all react the same way. You will want to tailor your punishment—if you need to use it at all—to the individual child, and not impose the same kind and amount on all.

In a friendly household, punishment and penalties are not needed most of the time because most children try to co-operate. They respond more readily when they are treated fairly and as distinct individuals and praised more often than criticized.

Conflict is inevitable—and healthy

Though a child may try to be co-operative this does not mean that he will never question or resist your authority. Some conflict is not only inevitable, it is healthy. A child who never shows a spark of independence—or rebellion—but always toes the line will in the end find it difficult to stand on his own two feet. To be able to develop a sense of right and wrong of his own, a child needs to have faith in himself and his judgment. What parent wants his child to grow up to be the kind of person who blindly follows a leader, or who always goes along with the crowd because he lacks self-confidence and inner strength? Children who have developed a healthy self-esteem are bound to assert themselves—you would not want it any other way.

Sometimes this self-assertion is hard to cope with, there's no question about that. The Blackstones would be the first to tell you so. Their eleven-year-old Nick was getting more insolent by the day, it seemed. And his comings and goings were top secret. Up till now, he had been confiding and amiable, but these days he never bothered to explain where he was going or what he was going to do. And he was always insisting, "All the *other* kids are allowed to stay out until after nine o'clock," or, "All the *other* guys are going to the movies tonight," or, "The *other* boys don't have to do chores after school."

While Nick's parents knew that this stage of relying on his friends' authority and pitting that authority against theirs was a natural step in his development, they didn't just grin and bear it. Nor did they discard their notions of right and wrong by letting him run wild and giving in to his every request. They did overlook a lot of routine annoyances—Nick's sloppy dress, for instance, and his messy room—so that they would not have to nag at him all the time. They knew that beneath his occasional defiance, Nick still needed their love and approval and valued their opinions.

During the early teens extra doses of parental patience and understanding are needed to keep conflicting ideas from flaring into family explosions. *How* do you discipline a fifteen-year-old girl who insists that all her friends stay out at least until midnight on dates and at parties? The Everetts for example, want their Ann home by eleven at the latest. She is not to have dates except on Saturday nights. Ann thinks her parents are unreasonable for not letting her stay out until midnight or go to a party on an occasional Friday. Her point of view deserves consideration. Many such situations call for family discussions rather than orders and inflexible rules and regulations.

Teen-agers around Ann's age frequently complain that their parents treat them as though they were much younger than they really are. Adolescents want to select their own clothes, make their own plans, choose their own friends. They are bound to make mistakes now and then, but these mistakes are necessary if they are to learn to take care of themselves and to become responsible members of society. You owe it to your teen-ager to keep him from making a serious mistake, but at the same time he needs your encouragement on this last lap to adulthood. That includes giving him many opportunities to assume the responsibility that goes with freedom. He needs more (not fewer) decisions that he can appropriately make; more chances to test himself out; more discussions of what can and cannot be done and why; fewer absolute prohibitions, and some very firm "No's" when the need for them is clear-cut and necessary.

Teen-agers welcome controls

Teen-agers may not say so, but they welcome your setting sensible limits for them. They want also to be respected as young people with some life of their own. You probably wonder why a fifteen-year-old, for example, often rebels if he really wants some limits set. Compare his with that of a young child. You have often seen three-year-old's making a great fuss about coming into the house when called. But have you noticed that they often seem relieved when they finally are picked up and carried in? Fifteen or three, all children can afford to protest when they can count on understanding parents to see that certain reasonable standards are upheld.

How you set limits has a great deal to do with how your teen-ager will accept them. When you talk to him as a person, rather than as a young child who still needs a good deal of direction, you stand a reasonable chance of getting his wholehearted co-operation. Your teen-ager is more likely to ask for, and accept, your friendly guidance when he knows that you are backing him up in his desire for eventual independence. Toward the end of adolescence he will be ready to take over his own discipline.

The sum and substance of discipline

At any age, successful discipline is never a method for manipulating youngsters to do your bidding. It is neither coercion, nor drill, nor humiliation, nor punishment. It does entail being "in charge" of your children without abusing your authority. Good discipline, which paves the way to self-discipline, allows a child self-respect while he learns respect for the rights and feelings of others. It gives him support, as well as encouragement and freedom to learn—and to learn from his mistakes. It helps him to develop responsibility for himself and to discipline himself. And self-discipline, as we have pointed out earlier, is the cornerstone of all ethical behavior.

Chapter four

THE SCHOOL AND YOU

Practically before you know it, your child is ready for school. Even for youngsters with some nursery-school experience a new world lies ahead—new friends, new challenges, new concerns. And, of course, parents are concerned, too—not only about how their children will do in school academically, but what the effects of these new influences, this new climate, will be. Will the teacher be patient and understanding, they wonder. Will she be too hard on the children? Or too easy? Will she play favorites? Will she like *my* child? And what about the school? Is it doing a good enough job, not only with subject matter but with the children's total development? Will it help them discover their abilities and make the most of them? Is the widespread criticism of American education justified? And today even mothers and fathers of six-year-olds worry about whether their youngsters will get into college!

Development of ethical behavior is on parents' minds, too. How much can the school teach about right and wrong How will the school's values and ideals help shape their child's future? What about the new children he will meet? One set of parents may have a few worries about Johnny's new friend, for example, whose family's ways seem so different from their own. Or Mary's chum who speaks with such a strange accent.

How much help?

You have already done a lot of "educating" long before your youngster ever entered school. Your child would not be ready for school today if you had not helped him in hundreds of ways up to now. By encouraging his attempts at independence, you have enabled him to be away from you for part of the day. Such routines as going to the washroom, using a handkerchief, and managing his outer clothing will not be major problems for him once he is at school. The opportunities you have given him to play with other children help him fit more easily into the school group. And because you have steered a middle course between overpermissiveness and overstrictness, he will have little difficulty in accepting the teacher's discipline if it also is firm and friendly. In short, you have been there all along backing him up. He still wants and needs your help, and will for a long time to come.

65

In a simple sense, he still needs a lot of help in just getting started off to school—but may think it babyish to be helped in public. Without reminders (and even with them) he may rush out excitedly to catch the school bus or catch up with the friends he walks to school with, forgetting the very lunch box he insisted that you buy the day before. Shoelaces may still defeat him, and he may lose his pennies for milk with exasperating regularity. Yet he may react fiercely to well-meant suggestions on your part. In the morning rush to find rubbers and mittens you may wonder dazedly, "Who helps him find things in school?"

One answer is—no one else, quite as much. The lost-and-found department for the primary grades is a busy and crowded one at the beginning of school. After a few months, business slacks off surprisingly, for most children who are expected and encouraged to become self-reliant usually do so, sooner or later. You have discovered this in many small ways already. Nature is on the children's side, and their own growth process helps. They become *able*—they begin to notice more, hear more, learn more. Then, too, there is that challenge—the fun of discovering: *I can do. I remember. I can learn. I am getting big.*

When to step in

Some children are helped best by parents who just stand back and let nature take its course because things are going so well. Some need parents who give nature a little assist from time to time—by raising standards of behavior or by frequent reassurance. Some need even more help, and many other kinds, if they are to negotiate the bridge between home and that outside, bigger life successfully. The growth and progress of *all* children is uneven. The better you know your child, and his place in his own age-group development, the surer your judgment can be when it comes to deciding "what to do when."

At the very start most children take to school eagerly. They are curious, they want to learn, they feel important. They enjoy the decisions they must make and the experiences they must face. They are expected to measure up, and they feel good when they do.

But some school beginners are timid about new places, new faces, new noises. They may not adapt so readily or enjoy it so obviously. But for them, too, accomplishment is just as important, acceptance in this new bigger world just as vital. They are apt to be the "worriers," or they may be the shy ones, for whom even a "baby step" requires serious thought and planning, and then a final surge of confidence and courage. Given plenty of support and understanding, both at home and in school, they, too, will grow and gain the satisfactions and strengths they need.

Six-year-old Prudy Kort needed—and got—just such support and understanding when, after a week at school, she simply refused to return. At first her mother could not understand it. Prudy had been looking forward eagerly to school and had come home the first few days bursting with enthusiasm and importance. But during that same time her three-year-old brother Ken became ill and required a good deal of Mrs. Kort's attention.

When the Korts discussed the sudden change in Prudy's attitude with their pediatrician, he pointed out how jealous Prudy was of the extra time and attention Ken was getting. He suggested that Mrs. Kort might get someone in to help for a little while with Ken before and after school so that she could have more time for Prudy. This difficult situation poses problems for a mother who naturally must tend to the needs of the child with an obvious physical illness, but Mrs. Kort was alert to Prudy's needs, even though she was worried about Ken. She did manage to get some extra help and to find time (and strength) to give Prudy more attention, even to accompany her to school and to stay for an hour each morning. Prudy's teacher was understanding, and the school was co-operative. By the end of the first week Prudy announced that her mother could stay home. She, Pru, now wanted to go to school—and by herself, too.

School phobia

Not all children who, like Prudy, suddenly change from loving school to fearing or hating it respond so readily. Nor is the solution always arrived at so easily. "School phobia," as it is termed, is really a misnomer. It is not school that these youngsters are afraid of, it is separation from their parents. This is why blindly pushing a child back to school only increases the trouble. A child can be terrorized into going, but he will hate it, and he will be paralyzed by his hate.

Easing a child's fear of separation will ease his fear of school. Sometimes this can be accomplished by reassuring the youngster in all the ways at your command that you do love him very much, that you will not be gone when he returns from school. Giving him small rewards as a token of his "grown-upness" may be helpful. But if all your patient and sympathetic measures fail, then turning for expert assistance without too much delay is indicated. Any error a parent may make can be repaired and undone except one—blind obstinacy that has to prove its rightness even at the child's expense. Since continued absence from school only intensifies the child's difficulty, with his dread of going back usually increasing as time goes on, child-guidance clinics generally give priority to these cases.

Self-discovery in school

But for most children school is exciting, and one of the exciting things school life has to offer them is self-discovery—learning about themselves as individuals, separate and distinct from the family. Most children enjoy this new identity which school opens up to them. Here is a place where they are no longer Ellen's little brother or Mommy's and Daddy's little girl. True, youngsters forfeit some of the favored treatment or concessions that make home so nice to come back to, but the new adventures of school—and the children's own exciting new identity—usually outweigh these. Independence can be a delightful and heady experience.

For parents the experience may be heady, but not so completely delightful. Primary-graders often become remarkably bossy and contradictory at home. They make some parents feel suddenly deprived of authority and frustrated in their efforts to "help."

You can accept this phase more easily when you realize that your youngster is not "resigning" from the family or rejecting its standards of conduct just because he is so eager to accept other authorities—and their ways of doing things, as well. When he contradicts, or stamps his foot in anger and protest, or even says belligerently, "But you don't know," he does not mean it quite the way it sounds. He has found out that in his wider world other people knew things, too. There are some new authorities in his life, ones he wants to please and be accepted by—his teacher, his new friends, his own school group.

Changing schools

What if you must send your first-grade child to a school where the rules seem too rigid and the policies unenlightened? Parents are sometimes faced with this situation, especially if their children have gone to nursery school or kindergarten where the program and atmosphere were friendly and relaxed. No child should have to attend a school that is not geared to his growth and to his needs, and you will want to work with others to try to effect changes. But what about your youngster in the meantime?

You certainly are not unsympathetic with him, and you do not want to be. At the same time you want neither to deny your own beliefs nor to undermine your child's confidence in his school. How can you help him best?

Suppose your child asks, "Why do we have to sit still in school? Why can't we move around?" You can tell him quite truthfully that it certainly would be more pleasant to do so, but that perhaps it is not practical. The class is probably large, and if everyone moved around all the time, then no one could hear the teacher. That is one reasonable explanation that a child can accept with your help. He is struggling right now to fit into two worlds, school and home. He needs to feel an important part of both settings, the school group just as much as the family. If you force a breach between your child and his school, you will only make life more difficult for him. But if you openly support a teacher who is being unfair, you make a breach between your child and you.

The difficult teacher

Mrs. Belden was faced with just such a problem. Her first-grader, Joy, had been happy in school the previous year. But this term something was very wrong—Joy had even cried once or twice before getting off in the morning. She didn't want to talk about it, but her mother encouraged her to tell her what was the matter.

"I don't like Mrs. Clark," Joy finally told her. "She makes us keep very quiet all the time, and she is always scolding us. She never explains when we don't understand something—it just makes her mad. I'm really afraid of her, Mom."

Joy's mother learned from other parents that a good deal of what her youngster complained of was true. The principal had not been able to help much, the teacher shortage being what it was, and the Beldens could not send Joy to another school. Mrs. Belden knew that Joy's first-grade experiences could color her whole attitude toward learning and that she had to help Joy cope with the situation and build up her confidence as well as her interest. She knew, too, that as Joy grew older she would meet other Mrs. Clarks in this world.

She decided to talk it out with her: "Joy, dear, you've seen me act cross and Daddy get angry once in a while when we're tired or upset. Some people, unfortunately, are more or less permanently cross and angry. They're not as friendly as we are—maybe they have lots of troubles. I don't know what's really bothering Mrs. Clark, but we'll just have to make the best of it for this term. One thing I'm sure of is that it's not you who's causing her to be angry. It is not your fault that she's cross."

Mrs. Belden did more to make life easier for Joy. She saw to it that she had friends with whom she could play as noisily and energetically as she liked. She planned some real projects with her at home. She even arranged occasional visits to out-of-the-way places. She read interesting books to her, and she also bought her a few simple ones that she was ready for. All this helped keep Joy's curiosity alive and stimulated her interests. It made her feel good about herself, too.

Mrs. Belden realized that there was no point in belittling Mrs. Clark. She helped Joy get all the good there was from school. She did not place her at the center of a tug of war between home and school, nor make her feel that she had only the family to depend on for satisfactions. Joy's parents did not pretend that there were no difficulties at school, and they talked about some of the things they would like changed. It was not an easy term, but it was no disaster. Mrs. Belden was successful in keeping up Joy's morale and helping her to be comfortable about school and interested in it.

71

All children want to feel comfortable about school, and you can help your child best by continuing to provide him with a relaxed and accepting home environment and a sympathetic and understanding awareness of what his outer world has become. Because school presents him with many new challenges, it can be a great comfort to him if the challenges implicit in family life—especially those involving either younger or older sisters and brothers—are kept to a minimum. You go a long way toward reducing these home challenges when you avoid making comparisons as to achievement, ability, looks, or anything else that might be worrisome—and such comparisons are always worrying to children.

If you know that things are going reasonably well, but find that your youngster is worrying about whether he will ever understand "numbers," for example, it will comfort him if you can dredge up your own memories of any difficulty at school. Offer your experience for laugh value to relieve tension. You can usually wind up such an anecdote with a cheerful, "And then I learned to do it!" or even a rueful (but truthful), "I never did get it quite right, but I grew up anyway!"

It is reassuring to children to learn that one survives, in spite of failure or embarrassment and that there are many ways to succeed in life without measuring up to every outside, or preconceived, standard. One good way to communicate this sensible self-acceptance is to take an easy attitude toward the whole business—perhaps to imply, "We do our best in things because we want to; we don't worry ourselves to pieces if we don't do as well as *everyone* in *everything*."

Abilities have a way of rising agreeably to the surface in such an atmosphere. Children who accept the fact that not everyone is liked by *everyone*, nor expected to do well in *everything*, usually manage later on to single out those they want most to be liked or admired by and the things they want most to do.

Some parents find it hard to offer their children this kind of reassurance. Often it is because as adults they are still trying to measure up to cloudy or difficult standards once set for *them*. One cannot go back again, but life does have a way of coming full circle. When similar demands are faced by one's offspring, there may be a real need to "meet them this time or bust!"

Why not occasionally ask yourself: "Will my child really have to do this or be that? Is what seemed right for me necessarily going to be best for him? Do I have to prove myself now by forcing my child to do something that I was unable to do when I was little?"

A rigidly preformed outline of what your child ought to be or to accomplish is dangerous—it is like expecting him to fit comfortably and walk and run with ease in the shoes of someone else, worn long ago. When you are flexible about your goals, proud of your youngster's accomplishments, and realistic about how much progress he is making —regardless of where it stacks up on any given month or Monday—he can capitalize and make new gains. And he will enjoy his progress just as much as you do in your stand-by-and-cheer position.

But in many places today there is not so much reason to stand by and cheer the schools. Many are overcrowded and understaffed, many school buildings are far from adequate. In some places the quality of teaching is poor, and the newer knowledge of how children grow and develop and learn is reflected neither in the curriculum nor in the handling of the youngsters.

But not all the criticism leveled at our schools is by any means justified. Many teachers and administrators are doing magnificent jobs. Their goals for children are the same as yours: informed, confident, courageous young people with a clearly developed sense of right and wrong. Schools have been blamed for many things, often unfairly. They cannot be expected to solve all of a child's difficulties, but it is worth noting that understanding teachers have helped many youngsters overcome their problems.

Judge a school fairly

Primary schools have changed so much during the past few years that even young parents cannot always judge them fairly on the basis of their own experience. When Mrs. Shiffman visited Barbara's classroom, she was amazed to find that not all the children were doing the same things. Some were building, some painting, some working on their numbers. The teacher was not just sitting at her desk. She was moving around the room freely from one group to another. It delighted Mrs. Shiffman to see how enthusiastic the children were about what they were doing. The teacher told her that one reason was that the children had had a part in the selection and planning of their activities. Thinking it over, Mrs. Shiffman decided that this might be a good cue for her at home.

Many present-day teachers, like present-day parents, know that learning occurs best and most easily in an atmosphere of warmth and security and freedom. In such an atmosphere, well-planned school programs provide youngsters with stimulating opportunities to put many of their own ideas into practice. These programs give girls and boys appropriate chances to assume responsibility, to become more independent, to learn to wait when it is necessary, to work co-operatively with others—all as they are acquiring skills and knowledge.

You can help your child by being active in school affairs

Your being active in school affairs—to the extent you can manage despite other home, family, and work responsibilities—can help your child a lot. When he is a little older he may be embarrassed at your being around too much, especially if you are in plain sight. But right now he loves it. If you can spare a little free time occasionally for volunteer work, you might be called on to deal with one of these problems—perhaps to support the need for a library or gym, perhaps a sudden epidemic which depletes personnel and resources, or a plan to use parents in interesting volunteer assignments. At any rate, whether you are willing to supply cookies for a parents' meeting, help at a grade party, or assist with a safety program, you do get to know the school people your child comes in contact with, his classmates, and their parents, and feel more in touch with the situation generally. This gives you an additional common bond with your child, one of activity as well as natural interest. It keeps you and your child comfortably "in the know," and it may give him an added good feeling about himself to boot.

Mrs. Parks, busy with a job and a household, at first resented the individual conferences which had replaced the report card in Tommy's school. When she talked over her son's progress with his teacher, Miss Craig, she began to appreciate the value of such discussions. They talked about Tommy's interests and attitudes at home as well as at school, and each of them was able to get a fuller picture of Tommy and his needs. It was clear to Mrs. Parks that the teacher really understood Tommy. She felt so comfortable with Miss Craig that she even managed to tell her how she sometimes worried about whether Tommy was as bright as his cousin of the same age.

Miss Craig pointed out to her that Tommy was eager, interested, and doing very well indeed. She explained that what was important was how favorably Tommy's present progress compared with his past accomplishments, not how he stacked up against another child. Together, Mrs. Parks with her unique knowledge of her own child, and Miss

Craig with her special knowledge of the whole group, mapped out the best ways to help Tommy at home and at school. And Tommy, knowing that they were both on his side, reaped the benefits. He was able to tackle his schoolwork with more self-confidence and thus with more success.

Ernest Marx, at eight, had just moved with his family to a new town. He had loved his old school, which was a good one, and had hated to leave it. But he had always had lots of friends, and no one anticipated that he would have trouble in adjusting to new surroundings. It did not work out that way. After a month of seeing Ernest lonely, not being accepted into the group, and certainly not doing his best in school, Mrs. Marx decided to talk it over with his teacher. This proved to be a first-rate example of how parent-teacher co-operation pays off. The teacher suggested which boys would be best for the Marxes to invite to a special outing. She also followed up by assigning Ernest to a joint project with two of the boys his mother had asked over for dinner. She gave Ernest other opportunities in the classroom to work co-operatively with boys with similar interests. In no time at all, Ernest was no longer a "new" boy. He might eventually have been accepted on his own, but with his mother *and* his teacher co-operating, his path was smoothed, his interest in school was heightened, and he did not have to "sweat it out" alone.

Not all teachers and parents can see eye to eye on a particular problem. It would be naïve to think they could. Many parents cannot believe that any difficulty their children may be having at school can have any relationship to what is going on at home. It is easier for them to put all the blame on the teacher. And the teacher, who must do her best with a whole group of children, often feels that a little more parental attention would have avoided what appears to be a school problem. In conferences together, parents and teachers learn to understand and respect each other's roles. They talk not only about the child's schoolwork, but they discuss the "whole child" and how his needs can best be met at home and at school. Parent-teacher groups have been very successful in bringing about greater home-school co-operation and in helping to improve schools and school programs. In many communities they hold discussion meetings where all kinds of problems are freely aired and constructive plans for improvement can be formulated and carried out.

During these first school years, the teacher's kindness, understanding, and example will have an important influence on your child's ethical growth. Her kindness and understanding will help him in his adjustment to his new and bigger world. How she treats him and the other children will give him a preview of how all people are to be treated. A teacher who talks about democracy but practices discrimination in the classroom cannot help but do serious damage to a child's ethical development. The child may learn that it is not so bad to poke fun at a member of a minority if at the sime time he proclaims aloud that tolerance is an important virtue. Later on, he may even seek to ingratiate himself with a group that jeers at minorities by doing it himself, bribing his conscience by using the "words" of tolerance. This is one additional reason for your being in close touch with the school situation, to learn what the attitudes are, and to make your own standards and practices clear.

The older child in school

Thus far we have seen examples only of younger children and their early school experiences. Now let us take a look at eleven-year-old Joey Gold. He has been in school for nearly six years. He has mastered many skills, he has lots of friends, he has come along fine. But you would not know it to listen to him—he would rather admit to any-thing than to say he likes school. To him and to his pals, saying that school is fine is as unheard of as asking for a reduction in their allowances.

All this does not trouble the Golds too much because Joey not only gets along well with his schoolmates, he also does well in his studies. And they are not bothered when he says, "Oh, our teachers are O.K., but they don't know so much." Joey and his boy friends are quick to note—and comment on—any and all deficiencies, both real and imagined, of their teachers (and parents). And they cannot always turn off their restlessness and preadolescent need to rebel once they enter the classroom. But they are eager for knowledge, interested in practically everything, and have a great desire to be useful and important.

Parents and teachers alike can find many ways to capital-ize on these qualities. These youngsters already show many evidences of a strong sense of right and wrong. When they have chances to work out problems with one another, for example, they are remarkably clear about what is fair and just. By taking some of their antics in stride, as the Golds did with Joey, respecting their struggles to grow up, not expecting more of them than is really possible, but not being content with less, schools and home can help pre-adolescents move ahead with confidence.

It was not quite so simple for Martin Stone, Joey's twelve-year-old cousin. Like Joey, Martin had always done well, but this semester in a new school he suddenly lost all interest and did very poorly indeed. His parents tried to help him all they could, but they finally realized that this was no passing phase that Martin would outgrow. Under-standing though they tried to be, they knew he was going to need more help than they and the teachers could give him. They decided to seek outside professional guidance.

Martin was helped to get at the root of what was contributing to his present difficulties. In his new and more demanding school. Martin's failure to be elected an officer of the Science Club had been interpreted by him as total rejection by the other boys, even though outwardly at the time he appeared to be no more than normally disappointed. Coming, as it did, three months after the death of his beloved grandfather, this was too much for the previously well-accepted Martin to take. Fortunately, the Stones could plan for and welcome professional help, instead of blaming themselves or refusing to see that Martin had a real problem. Without help, he might well have continued to lag behind. He might never have been able to develop his really fine mind and his extraordinary potential as an intelligent, ethical human being.

Critical thinking about ethics

As youngsters move to the high-school level and prepare to take their places in an adult world, then self-discipline, knowledge, and responsibility take on a new and greater urgency. In good high schools critical thinking about ethical problems is encouraged. Good teachers can help their students distinguish between fact and biases and to investigate for themselves before they accept or reject any idea. Young people can and should be taught how to weigh all the facts, to think independently, to learn that it takes as much courage to disbelieve as to believe, and that neither blind belief nor blind disbelief is necessarily admirable. But many high schools today fall far short of accomplishing these goals. They have been accused of turning out youngsters who are half-educated, soft, conforming, with little regard for ethical conduct.

Perhaps some of these accusations are justified, but let us take a deeper look. In recent years how many Americans have grown smug and complacent, with a singular unwillingness to face hard facts? In many homes today, what is prized more, a new car or a new idea? A new painting or a new color TV set? Who is admired more, the man, however ruthless, who can put over a big deal, or a dedicated college professor? Until parents are willing to demand more of themselves, until they themselves put a higher value on intellectual excellence and on ethical behavior, they cannot fairly place the entire blame on the schools or on the teachers.

Parents often expect teachers to be superior human beings. While parents want school people to be intelligent, emotionally mature, and creative, they balk at paying what it costs to attract persons of such caliber to the field. Concern for what and how children are taught, for funds for education, for enough teachers and classrooms, for salary levels, for adequate school buildings—this is the business of every parent. Joining together with others in parent-teacher groups, civic clubs, citizens' committees is a responsibility all parents must be willing to take on.

Some parents, concerned about the public high schools, enter their youngsters in private secondary schools. While many of them would prefer not to send their children to private schools, they are equally reluctant to send them to overcrowded, and sometimes second-rate, public high schools. The cost is burdensome for many parents, but prizing what the better independent schools can provide for their youngsters, they willingly take on the extra financial load.

What frequently happens then is that these parents, often the most enlightened and education-conscious parents in a community, do not feel obliged to work to improve the public schools. But the folly of this must be apparent to anyone concerned with ethical behavior. Learning right from wrong and maintaining a democratic society depend on how *all* parents act as responsible citizens and on what they do to provide good schools for *all* youngsters, not on the quality of education for the few. No matter what schools youngsters attend, they will all eventually live and work together in a community and form its strength and its future. By allowing any children to have substandard education, to be deprived and neglected, and to run the risk of their becoming hostile, unethical adults is to defeat our democratic ideal.

Academic training is not enough

Parents and teachers know that all children, from high school seniors down to first-graders, learn best (at home as well as at school) when they are respected for themselves and their accomplishments and are helped to feel capable and worthwhile. What do home and school consider the real goals of education? Certainly respect for learning, a mastery of subject matter, and an acquiring of skills are some of the goals. But those responsible for children want even more than all these, important as these goals are. What good are knowledge and skills to a youngster if he has no inner strength and security? More than acquiring book learning, parents and teachers want their young people to understand themselves and others. They want them to be able to go through life without hurting themselves or others. Parents want their children to know the difference between right and wrong and to have the courage to live by their convictions. The kind of education aimed at achieving these results is what all young people deserve. It is a joint product of home and school.

As you know, many schools are doing a remarkable job, although far too many are not. But how and what the schools teach is largely a response to how and what parents want their youngsters to learn and what they are willing to pay for. While it is heartening to note that curriculum changes, special kinds of classes, new teaching methods, and improved ways of dealing with youngsters are taking place in schools in every part of our country, they are not occurring in enough places nor with enough speed to permit complacency. We are all aware that there are serious shortcomings in many of our schools, but practically none of them is past correction if we acknowledge them, and if we work hard and seriously—and fast—to overcome them. Only in so doing can we truly help our youngsters develop into responsible, enlightened, ethically mature citizens.

Chapter five

MURDER IN THE

LIVING ROOM

Studies—or, at the very least, opinions—on the effects of commercial television on children are almost as numerous as television sets themselves. More than that, they come in nearly as many sizes and models. Some accuse certain programs of actually causing juvenile delinquency, while others defend TV viewing as a stimulus to children's reading. Still others state that what is needed are simply more studies. "Not enough data are in to determine the effects of TV on children," run several widely quoted conclusions.

What stand to take about television

No wonder many conscientious parents are confused about what to think or what stand to take. Eager for more conclusive findings, they are nevertheless not content to wait indefinitely for clinical and statistical evidence. Logic and reason tell them that there must be some relationship between most run-of-the-mill TV fare and their children's ethical values.

In the face of a steady diet of TV murder and violence, how can a child learn to distinguish right from wrong? What does it mean to him to see brutality offered up as entertainment? To see human life held cheap? To learn that crime does not pay, but only if one gets caught before the final commercial? How can a child reconcile the debased values portrayed for him right in his own living room with those his parents have taught him to cherish?

Perplexed by these questions, many parents are still uncertain about whether to ban or curtail TV programs of questionable merit. And their youngsters, sensing no real parental conviction, put up stiff arguments, and generally win out. Why this lack of conviction? Perhaps one of the reasons is the very newness of the medium. Parents had no TV when they were young, and consequently no rules from their own childhood exist to guide them. While they may feel perfectly secure in setting up reasonable rules about bedtime or about how much candy is too much, they are often at sea about what to do about controlling or rationing television.

This uncertainty showed itself clearly in the Farmer household. Seven-year-old Pete was an avid viewer of TV detective stories and Westerns, though no more so than most of the other youngsters in the neighborhood. Mrs. Farmer thought his absorption in all the killing and shooting was excessive, but, after all, hadn't she read that these programs drained off a child's hostility and were probably healthy? Still, it did not seem to work out that way. Pete and his friends were, if anything, more violent and aggressive in their play—not less so—after watching their favorite shows.

Parents are not therapists

The whole notion that hostility can be siphoned off by viewing it on TV stems from a misapplication to child-rearing of a technique in psychoanalytic therapy. (See Chapter III, *Spare the Child*, p. 44.) But a parent is not a therapist whose job it is to treat a child who is already sick. A parent must teach his child right from wrong by helping him to learn socially acceptable ways of discharging his aggressive and destructive tendencies.

Pete and his friends do not need several hours a day of vicarious murder and violence to satisfy their aggressive longings, even if it were true that such TV programs accomplish this. Occasional shows of this kind may do no harm, but a steady diet serves no useful purpose. On the contrary, these programs can confuse a child, lower his standards, and suggest to him that most people put a small value on human life.

Latest statistics on the amount of out-of-school TV viewing by elementary-school children reveal that these youngsters average almost twenty-three hours a week—*about the same amount of time as most of them spend in school.* High-school youngsters average somewhat less, around twelve hours. (In this chapter we are concerned with the effects of television on youngsters from three to thirteen. By three, many children are already TV fans; by thirteen, their sense of reality is usually clearly established and their critical values more highly developed.)

No one knows how much time preschoolers spend plunked down before TV sets, but the general impression is that it is considerable. Some mothers report that their three-year-olds make a beeline for the set right after they climb out of bed in the morning and watch for hours and hours. Youngsters of this age are unable to make clear-cut distinctions between what is real and what is not, and there are very few good programs today designed especially for them. Many young children are frightened but fascinated by what they hear and see, and they keep right on going back for more, despite their fears. It is the clear duty of parents to restrict their young children's TV viewing. Surely they cannot expect these youngsters to have more sense than they have!

The electronic nursemaid

Preschoolers need lots of activity to help them learn and grow. Sitting still for hours in front of a TV set is not good for them, even if there were a substantial number of programs tailored to their age for them to look at. Their favorites are cartoons and commercials, but they will watch anything else they are permitted to. The temptation to allow them to park themselves in front of the TV set is great, especially as it gives mothers a chance to get on with their housework or have a quiet chat with a friend while their youngsters are being tended by this electronic nursemaid. But when mothers realize that much of what their children watch can be frightening to them and that continuous TV viewing is extremely unwise, they will regulate carefully what their youngsters look at and for how long. In this area, just as in others we have been discussing, your child needs and welcomes your firm and friendly protection.

Tommy Warring's father pooh-poohed the effects of television on his five-year-old son. He often told his wife, "My mother used to read bedtime stories to me when I was his age that were twice as scary as the stuff he sees on TV. They didn't bother me any."

But when Tommy started to wake up several nights a week frightened and crying, Mr. and Mrs. Warring decided to talk the whole matter over with their pediatrician. After eliminating other possible causes, the doctor asked them about Tommy's TV habits. The boy did watch a fair number of programs, and sometimes, according to his mother, he gave the impression that he thought at least two of his favorite TV characters were real.

This essential difference—the frankly made-up fairy tale world and television's simulated real world—was what Mr. Warring had failed to realize. The fairy stories *his* mother had read to him made no attempt to depict reality and therefore he as a youngster had found little difficulty separating the fantastic world from the one he actually lived in.

But Tommy's television world was not the same. Seeing and hearing a moving image on the screen carries much greater impact than being read a make-believe story. For one thing, while listening to the fairy tale the child is protected by the limits of his own imagination. Not everything is spelled out and made to appear lifelike. For another, his mother is there to reassure him that this is all "just pretend" if he seems frightened. And she and he can both tell each other how much they dislike the bad character and are against his wrongdoing.

When the Warrings understood the very real difference in impact between make-believe stories and too real TV, they called a halt to the unsuitable programs Tommy had been watching. Very soon his fears began to subside, and his nightmares occurred with less and less frequency. Mrs. Warring did not simply *subtract* unsuitable TV programs from Tommy's life; she *added* stimulating activities. She took Tommy and his friends to visit the Indian museum, planned some real projects with them, and even encouraged them to put on a little play of their own.

Do you approve of crime?

Parents who find it easy to regulate their younger children's TV viewing habits sometimes act resigned when it comes to their school-age youngsters. While they deplore the appalling amount of violence and crime their children are exposed to, they seldom do, or even say, anything about it. And if parents show no disapproval, they cannot expect their youngsters to feel any. But because you are seriously concerned with your child's ethical development, it is up to you to take a strong moral stand.

How can parents expect a youngster to be revolted by shooting, violence, and killing if his parents tacitly approve of this daily barrage of brutality, complete with sight and sound? How can a child accept fully the important ethical principle that it is wrong to hurt another person if the programs he sees teach him over and over again to take pride in violence and to be ashamed of sympathy or almost any tender feeling? Isn't it possible that a child who is exposed repeatedly to sadism is in danger of losing his revulsion to it? Or even perhaps, at some level, of growing to like it? Isn't there the chance that he may acquire another set of values, debased and vulgar, surely not the ones you want for him? What about a child who sees thousands of screen murders right in his own living room from the time he is six until he is twelve? Can he remain completely unaffected? Will he find it easy to consider human life sacred and its destruction tragic?

All of this does not mean that the crime and violence on TV are capable of eventually turning your child into a delinquent. Delinquency is more complex than that, and as we have pointed out earlier, your child acquires his basic standards and values from you. A child who loves his parents and has strong ties to them is not likely to repudiate their teachings easily, but through a steady diet of TV crime and violence he runs the very serious risk of blunting his moral sensibilities. He may possibly get the impression that brutality is widespread, killing as common as running an errand, and guns part of every he-man's equipment. We have finally learned that violence is not the best way to settle differences, but most of the blood-and-thunder TV shows children watch today teach them that it is the *only* way.

Does television clarify life?

Of course you will speak your mind, make your own attitudes clear, and leave your children in absolutely no doubt as to what you think about the brutal acts they have seen glorified on the TV screen. But the effectiveness of your teaching and example can be reduced considerably if what your children are continually exposed to not only fails to support, but indeed contradicts, you.

At a recent parents' meeting to discuss television's effects on children, one parent took a stand in favor of violence. Mr. Green put it this way:, "I don't want Betty to grow up thinking the world is absolutely marvelous, that there's no violence in it. She might as well learn about life as it is from watching TV." Betty's father was sure he was right, but it did not take long for other parents to convince him otherwise.

"Last night I decided to watch TV with the kids," one mother told him. "I made up my mind to find out what they were looking at and how they took it. Before the evening was over, we had seen five shootings, one man viciously beaten, another knifed, and a third brutally kicked. Do you really think that kind of thing prepares your Betty for life as she will know it?"

Before the meeting was over, most of the parents had agreed to limit their children's TV viewing and to make their own position strong and clear.

Protection is not censorship

The ugly word "censorship" had been raised during the meeting. It was as unsettling to some fathers and mothers as the term "judgmental" to which we referred in the first chapter. Parents must ignore this kind of nonsense. If protecting children from evil is assailed by some as censorship, most conscientious parents can go right ahead and censor, secure in the knowledge that it is their responsibility to guard their youngsters from undesirable influences. How many of you would invite a gangster into your house to entertain your children? Yet his real-enough-to-be-believed TV counterpart is a constant visitor who stays around even longer than The Man Who Came to Dinner.

The widespread notion that TV crime and violence affect only unhappy children or those already predisposed to get into difficulties bears looking into. As every parent knows, teaching a child right from wrong and bringing him up to be strong and healthy is no simple job. There are times when *all* children are unhappy, vulnerable to a greater degree, more susceptible to harmful influences. Things that are evil are evil, and every responsible parent has a duty to spare his child from potential damage of any kind. And, of course, the child who is already troubled is especially susceptible to TV crime and violence. Instead of stealing an apple or breaking a window, for example, he might "mug" an old man. Is it arguable that because a child is already disturbed, he should be allowed to be disturbed further—that it is all right to stimulate and intensify his cruel and aggressive fantasies?

At this point it seems a good idea to recall the following from an earlier chapter:

What exactly do we mean by right and wrong—by wanting children to be good and to grow up to be good? Not merely that they be well-mannered, though parents wouldn't mind a touch more of that! Certainly not that they be blindly obedient. Not simply that they stay neat and clean, though that would be fine when it's appropriate. And decidedly not that they remain docile and unquestioning. By teaching children right from wrong we mean helping them up the slow, gradual path to ethical behavior. And what is ethical behavior based on? On deep feelings of love and sympathy, of justice and fairness, of courage and loyalty.

90

Does this sound like a tall order? Of course it does. But it is certainly the kind of behavior that parents want their children to develop.

Just a minute's reflection will tell you how much harder this "tall order" becomes if without protest you allow your youngsters to be constantly assaulted—year in and year out —with programs that glorify the exact opposite of all these feelings.

The myth that television keeps a family together

We must look with skepticism also on the frequently made claim that television is good for families because it keeps them together. Again that ubiquitous and uncritical "togetherness"! Can any sensible person really believe that family unity is strengthened—that any significant interaction takes place—when all its members are staring straight ahead at some screen holocaust? This is not to deny that parents and their children do have fun together watching some special or favorite programs, and that these shows sometimes even spark conversation and stir up discussion. But good family relationships do not come from passively sitting back watching TV. They depend, as you know, on mutual love and respect, on the spirit that parents create, on a genuine sharing of interests and responsibilities.

Some parents have a tendency to make television a convenient scapegoat on which to place blame for everything their children do or fail to do. One father complained that his son rarely read a book now that the TV set was a permanent fixture in the family living room. But when asked how many books the youngster read before that, he finally admitted, "Oh, about four a year." True, some of the dire predictions made back in the early days of TV have not materialized. Eyesight has not been ruined. Children pass or fail their school grades in the same proportion they did before TV, and those who always read a good deal still do. Those youngsters to whom reading was a chore—just something you had to do to get by in school—find TV a relief, a way to get the fun of a story without the work of reading it.

Help your child acquire taste

Not everything on TV falls into the crime and violence pattern, although too much of it does. Some programs are, at the least, in questionable taste and as yet there are not nearly enough worthwhile ones. If you let your preschooler see only what is suitable for him and if you introduce your older youngsters to those good programs that do exist—first-rate drama, sports events, documentaries, music, public affairs—you help them develop sound values and critical judgment. Your own TV tastes will have some effect on your children's viewing, but you cannot always expect your youngsters to agree with you on what constitutes good entertainment.

Taste is not acquired overnight, and you cannot force it. Belittling children's favorite programs is not the way to raise their sights. Some programs will obviously appeal to them more than to you. Some of the comedy shows, for example, that strike you as banal can be sidesplitters to them. There is much on television that is just plain fun, and few would insist that TV sets should be turned off permanently. But regulating the kinds of programs children see and how long they spend at it is another matter. When you are tolerant of your youngsters' present tastes, except for obviously harmful choices, and suggest that they, too, might want to look at what you think is worth seeing, you are encouraging them to widen their horizons.

When you keep track of what your children are viewing on TV (at home at least!), are firm about what is and is not permitted in the family living room, and state clearly why, you are registering your own standards. These are not lost on your youngsters—they serve as reminders of what standards you expect of them, even if they look at undesirable programs when visiting their friends or if they cannot resist tuning them in now and then on their own.

You perform an important service for your children—and for *all* children—when you protest programs featuring excessive violence and demand better ones. You can help keep the good programs on the air by expressing your interest in them. You can make your views known to the FCC, the networks, the advertising agencies, the sponsors. The law of the land says that the air waves belong to the people. Let us get them back—let them serve the people.

Chapter six

THOSE SCENE-STEALING

SIBLINGS

"There won't be any jealousy between our two," declared Agnes Brady the day before she brought the new baby home from the hospital. "We've really *prepared* Chris for all this . . . and we're not going to let this new sister of his steal the show."

How to prepare a child for a new arrival

The Bradys had done all the things that conscientious parents do to help a first child accept the coming of a new brother or sister. Knowing that with the new baby's arrival five-year-old Chris would have to step up to a new position in the family, they were determined to give him all the help he required to take this giant step. No longer would he be the one and only—soon he would have to share his parents' love with another. To make it easier for him, Mr. and Mrs. Brady decided to treat the arrival of the baby as a family affair, letting Chris share in some of the preparations. He chose a few of the baby's clothes and even helped his father paint the bassinet. Clearly he was enjoying his prebaby role.

When Mrs. Brady went to the hospital, Chris's grandmother, whom he was fond of, took care of him while his father was at work. His mother talked with him on the telephone for a few minutes each day during her hospital stay. Everyone saw to it that Chris was not made to feel neglected or, worse yet, rejected!

As soon as the Bradys brought the baby home, they deposited her in the nursery—and then turned all their attention to Chris. His mother gave him a big hug and a bigger present, and she told him how much she had missed him. His father spent most of his free time with Chris during the next few days and made a special point of it whenever his wife was occupied with the baby. In spite of all these well-meant (and necessary) efforts, imagine Mrs. Brady's surprise when, about two weeks later, Chris marched into the nursery and bopped his baby sister over the head with a rattle before his mother could stop him.

"Why, what's the matter, Chris?" she asked, "Don't you know the baby is *your* baby, too? Why would you want to hurt her?"

"It's no fun around here any more," Chris said glumly. "I wish you'd left her in the hospital."

Luckily, Mrs. Brady was able to summon up her good sense along with her sense of humor. Although she and her husband had done everything "just right," nonetheless the green-eyed monster had managed to invade the nursery. What in the world had gone wrong? Nothing, really. But like so many other parents, they had simply not wanted to face the inevitability of jealousy. After all, the baby wasn't really Chris's—she was a new member of the family who demanded much of Mrs. Brady's time. Like all children, Chris wanted not only to be loved, he wanted to be loved *best*.

You can't wish envy away

A young child has no way of knowing in advance that there will be enough love to go around. No amount of preparation or wise handling can completely eradicate envy, nor can it equip a first child for the painful experience of sharing parental love with a newcomer. True, parents can do much to minimize jealousy and to help their youngster convert angry feelings into constructive ones. Yet it is obviously impossible for each child in the family to have his parents' love exclusively—and learning to accept this fact of life is part of the growing-up process.

Mrs. Brady did not scold Chris for showing his perfectly natural feelings. Instead she let him know that she understood: "It was more fun for you when we were getting ready for the baby. But now she's really here and that's different. It makes you mad sometimes. I don't blame you a bit, dear, and I do love you just as much as ever."

By accepting Chris's mean feelings and letting him know she still loved him even when he was angry, Mrs. Brady made it easier for him to cope with his jealousy. Her understanding kept him from feeling ashamed. While she did not punish him, she let him know *unmistakably* that he could not hurt his little sister. He had a right to feel angry, she told him, but he would not be permitted to take it out on the baby. It took time and frequent reassurances in words and actions, but Chris did come to learn that his baby sister was no real threat to him—that there was love enough to go around.

Don't make it hard for the older child

Some families unwittingly make it hard for a first child to handle his jealousy. Take the Johnsons, for example. The day four-year-old Martha Johnson was introduced to her new baby sister was a far from happy occasion for her. Her mother and father seemed to have eyes and ears only for the new baby. Up till now Martha had been the apple of their eye. But as the days went by they just seemed to take her more and more for granted. Even the visitors—friends and relatives—seemed to think the new baby was the whole show.

To get her share of attention, Martha began acting like a baby herself. In hurt protest, she insisted on having a bottle occasionally, which her busier-than-ever mother took time to fix for her. Mrs. Johnson's work load increased still more when Martha began to wet the bed again at night. And the day Martha openly displayed her resentment by pinching her baby sister good and hard, Mrs. Johnson exploded. She scolded Martha severely, and sent her to her room. But later that evening when she talked with her husband about Martha's behavior, she realized she had not been taking Martha's feelings sufficiently into account. "I think she needs comfort and attention—not punishment," said Mr. Johnson. "We've been expecting her to grow up overnight. After all, she's used to being the baby. No wonder she's been acting up."

It took a while to perk up Martha's wilted self-esteem and convince her that she was still very much loved. The Johnsons realized that punishing her for behavior that stemmed from jealousy only made that jealousy more intense. They put a stop to that, and let Martha know they did not blame her for resenting the baby. Both of them told her in every way they knew that she was just as important to them as the new baby was. Her mother not only permitted her to act like a baby when she seemed to need to, but she also allowed her to do things that "babies can't do" —like staying up a little later at night to hear a story or listen to a record. Her father took her on some special Sunday outings. And while they naturally talked about the baby, they managed to demote her from first place on their Conversation Parade.

Her parents never gave Martha the notion that they were neglecting the baby on her account. Both her mother and father wanted her to realize that she could always depend on them to be fair to her as well as to the baby. Gradually, as Martha felt more certain of her own secure niche in the family, her need to act like the baby subsided and her resentment gave way to genuine co-operation. She actually enjoyed helping with the baby now and then. She felt like an important first assistant when she handed her mother a diaper or the safety pins or got the bottle out of the refrigerator—for the baby these days, not for herself!

Even older chilren find it difficult to share their parents' love. Take ten-year-old Pamela Golden. She had been an only child for so long that at first she was delighted with the idea of having a baby brother. But one day during the baby's second month, she said to her mother, "You just don't seem to have a minute for *me* anymore!"

Mrs. Golden was surprised at the intensity of feeling behind her daughter's words. For the past year, Pamela had not had much time for *her*. Like most ten-year-olds, Pam was busy a good deal of the time with her friends, and had many interests outside the family circle. Lately she had even seemed to be stepping up her away-from home activities and could hardly wait to be off with her girl friends. How ironic it was, Mrs. Golden thought, for Pamela to accuse *her* of neglect.

Then it began to dawn on Mrs. Golden that while Pam loved the baby, she was also jealous of him and was running away from her jealousy by intensifying her outside interests. Pamela simply had not realized that a new baby would require so much attention, and her mother had just taken it for granted that Pam would understand. The fact that the baby was a boy heightened Pam's jealousy and made her want continuing evidence of her parents' love for her —a girl! She needed to be certain that both her mother and father were still interested in her, in her school work, in all her other activities.

Mrs. Golden talked it over with her—explained that it was hard getting accustomed to having a baby in the house, but that she understood Pam's feelings. She reassured her, "There'll be more time for other things when I really get used to it all. Right now, I'll need your help and Daddy's help, too." Pamela came to learn that it required the co-operation of everyone in the family to make things go along smoothly. She found that girls were every bit as desirable as boys. When she was assured not only of her own warm and special place in her parents' affection but also of the very real value of her uniquely feminine contribution to the household, she no longer felt left out. Even a busy ten-year-old who has already begun to move away from home base has trouble giving up some of the limelight.

Fair play begins with siblings

Loves and hates which brothers and sisters feel for each other (and they exist side by side) are important experiences in their lives. Learning to get along with one another, to allow affection to triumph over jealousy prepares a child to get along with people outside the family later on. These are important building blocks in the development of ethical behavior. By acknowledging a young child's jealousy and helping him cope with it, parents encourage the positive feelings that exist within him so that, in the long run, those feelings can win out over the negative ones. On the face of it, this is no small assignment.

What about the rivalry of older children where there is no new baby in the family? Is continued friction natural? Inevitable? The Harwoods, for instance, claim that it is, and their two boys, aged eight and ten, actually fight a great deal of the time. "Show me the kids who never fight!" says Mr. Harwood. "It's natural for brothers to quarrel, get mad, and punch each other."

When Dave gets a new baseball mitt, his younger brother, Bob, demands one just like it—or Dave better watch out! If Bob gets a bigger piece of pie than Dave's, the fur flies. Both boys fight continually over who was given a special privilege or who was shortchanged.

While occasional conflicts can serve to get angry feelings out into the open and help youngsters work out compromises, a never-ending battle is a disruptive rather than a unifying force. When children like Dave and Bob are forever at swords' points, there are obviously reasons behind their behavior that bear looking into.

Nursery rivalries must end

The Harwoods might ask themselves if they are unwittingly doing something to encourage their sons' rivalry and fighting. Boys around Bob's and Dave's ages should have been helped long ago to express and resolve some of the natural jealousy which prevailed in their baby days. But by taking the position that this seething rivalry is just a normal part of family life, the Harwoods are failing to help their boys find mature solutions to their differences.

It is up to parents to encourage their children to resolve their differences without endless bickering and fighting. You do not want to add fuel to the flame by showing that you are either amused or flattered by signs of jealousy among brothers and sisters. And you need to make it clear that you expect them to outgrow their jealousies and infantile ways of expressing anger and to find civilized ways to work out conflicts. This, in a very large sense, is what a family is for!

Odious comparisons

Most adults still show traces of their early brother-sister conflicts and problems. Even when parents are careful not to compare one child with another, youngsters themselves often do. A child who grows up feeling that he is inferior to his older brother or sister may eventually just give up trying to succeed. A person who has always felt more capable than his sisters and brothers may assume that things will always come to him effortlessly. Another may harbor a feeling of guilt as a result of his too easy triumphs within the family.

While there are no sure-fire ways to resolve rivalries among brothers and sisters, parents can help to reduce friction when they themselves show no favoritism and do not pit children against each other. It helps to keep in mind that youngsters in the same family differ from one another in all sorts of ways. Margaret may be brighter than Jill, George handsomer than Al, Molly more lively than Charlotte, Joe more athletic than Paul. Even beyond these differences, no two children in the same family grow up in the same environment. The first-born lived for a while as an only child with parents who were inexperienced, possibly unsure of themselves. When the second child arrived, mother and father were older, maybe better off financially, perhaps even more mature emotionally. And parents' feelings may not be at all the same at the time each child is born.

While most parents do acknowledge that every child is unique and must be accepted for himself as he is, they sometimes forget that one child may need more praise and attention than another. The more certain you have helped each child to feel about his own worth, the less envious he will be of a brother or sister—the less he will need to vie for your affection. He can learn to appreciate and be proud of the talents or capabilities of his sisters and brothers.

Sometimes parents do like one child better than another and show it. Arthur Newburn, for example, was such a robust, smiling baby that everybody was attracted to him. He was a friendly outgoing toddler of two when his brother Jimmy was born. But Jimmy was scrawny and solemn faced. He lacked that certain spark that made Arthur so lovable and attractive. The Newburns had been looking forward to another son just like Arthur, but as the boys grew older, their differences became even more pronounced. Arthur was not only good looking, he was bright, talkative, and self-confident. Jimmy was subdued, shy, living always in the shadow of his gregarious, popular older brother. While Jim liked to read and try his hand at writing, Arthur made local history by becoming a star basketball player—just as his father had been when *he* was younger. Although the Newburns tried to be fair with both boys, they could never quite conceal their pride in Arthur and their disappointment in Jim. It was not until Jim went away to school—and away for the first time from his scene-stealing sibling—that he began to shine as a person in his own right. His interest in writing blossomed into a genuine flair for journalism, and he became editor of the school newspaper. Moreover, he made several good friends all on his own.

But Jim continues to be reserved and shy. He may well go through life feeling inadequate and resentful, in spite of all later achievements. Without help, the deep, smoldering anger Jim felt, but never dared show, may continue to plague his life in the years ahead.

There was plenty of envy in the Gillespie's home, too. Twelve-year-old Alice was painfully aware that her older sister Eileen was an honor student. After all, her parents were forever comparing the two girls' records. "Why can't you get grades like your sister's?" was the all-too-familiar refrain at home—and several of Alice's teachers echoed the theme. But Alice was more interested in art than in grammar and social studies. Besides, academic work was difficult for her. The constant comparisons hurt her self-esteem and made her deeply resent Eileen. Alice began to act sullen and un-cooperative and started to go around with a group of girls whose behavior was decidedly anti-school and anti-social as well. She took less and less interest in her work. Finally she came to a point where she was skipping school without her parents' knowledge.

Fortunately, the school psychologist was brought into the picture. He discussed the problem with Mrs. Gillespie and pointed out some of the causes and the significance of Alice's behavior. Together they agreed on a program to build up her self-esteem and to undo the damage that had already been done. Mrs. Gillespie realized that she had been expecting Alice to live up to standards way beyond her ability. Instead of continuing to compare her scholastic achievements—or lack of them—with those of her more successful sister, she encouraged Alice's other interests and talents.

With the co-operation of her art teacher, Alice entered a painting in a county-wide art contest. Her parents' praise of her efforts, together with subtle morale-boosting from her teachers, helped Alice feel worthwhile in her own right and capable of achievement. Of course her grades did not immediately improve, nor did she ever make the honor roll! But when pressure to compete with her sister was relieved, Alice began to show a good deal more interest in school. Her sessions with the psychologist proved extremely helpful. As her self-confidence began to grow, she became

more co-operative and friendly. Her what's-the-use attitude disappeared, and she began to take on the look of a
happy, loved youngster.

Believe in a child for what he is

In their eagerness to have their children excel and be a
credit to them, some parents make the mistake of measuring
one child against another. But this competitiveness on the
part of parents often boomerangs, causing a child to feel
that he must be something or somebody he is not to win his
parents' approval.

Each child needs to be valued for what he is and for
what he can do. Instead of being goaded to be what he is
not, he needs encouragement and appreciation for himself
as he is. By respecting a child for his individuality and
praising him for his own particular achievements, you help
to give him the self-confidence that will stimulate his
enthusiasm for living and learning. Brothers and sisters who
are valued for what they are, not compared unfavorably
with each other, can generally feel comfortable enough
about themselves to appreciate the efforts of others.

This ability to feel comfortable about yourself is an
important step in the development of ethical behavior. As
we have already pointed out, before a child can value
others, he must first be able to value himself. Life within
the family must teach him to value himself—to understand
something of his personal worth as well as his need for
others and their need of him. Ethical behavior is an affir-
mation of this positive attitude toward oneself and one's
fellow human beings.

The structure of today's family unit makes life less easy
for children in some ways than it used to be. Years ago,
family households were larger, with grandfathers and
grandmothers, uncles and aunts, living under the same roof
with children and grandchildren. Brothers and sisters received attention and love from several adults other than

their parents. When parents showed disapproval, children could go to a grandfather, an uncle, or an aunt for comfort, support, or advice. This frequently minimized their need to compete with one another for their parents' attention.

Today's smaller family groups, separated as they frequently are from relatives and intimate friends, tend to intensify rivalries and conflicts. That is why a child, especially as he grows older, often needs an adult "ally" outside the family with whom he can talk freely. Parents, too, find it useful to get together with other parents to talk out some of their common problems. In many communities there are discussion meetings and child study and parent education groups that provide ways to do so.

Apportion chores fairly

Thirteen-year-old Jo Ann Ryan, the oldest and only girl in a family of five, has a certain prestige which her younger brothers do not share. But she has a lot of household chores which she wishes they would share. Her mother relies on her as a part-time baby sitter and mother's helper, and Jo Ann is beginning to resent doing all that is expected of her. Although generally co-operative, she does feel burdened by all her family obligations. One day she told her aunt, who was visiting for the weekend, that no one ever let her have a minute to herself. "I'm *never, never, never* going to get married and have children!" she said. "Boys have it easy." Aunt Jane knew that Jo Ann was emoting, but there was justification in the girl's complaint. She decided to talk it over with Jo Ann's mother.

"Do you think perhaps you've been giving her too much responsibility just because she's the oldest and a girl?" she asked her sister. Mrs. Ryan had to admit that she had always taken Jo Ann's help for granted. When she stopped to evaluate the situation, she realized that there was no reason why she could not occasionally get someone in to help. Then she wouldn't be imposing on Jo Ann and curtailing some of the freedom which was rightfully hers. There was also no reason why the younger boys could not take over some of the chores that had gradually been delegated to their older sister.

It is not uncommon for a girl like Jo Ann to feel that it just doesn't pay to be a female when she sees that her brothers are having the best of it and that a major share of the responsibility for keeping the house and children in tow falls to her simply because she is a girl.

If chores and responsibilities are fairly apportioned among all the children, according to what can reasonably be expected of them, each can learn to do his share. Brothers and sisters need to learn to work together as a necessary part of family living. Working together for the common good strengthens family unity.

In large families, a reasonable amount of being in charge of the younger children provides valuable experiences for the older ones if they are not made to feel put upon. But when Mrs. Ellberg, for example, insists that eight-year-old Tony take his five-year-old brother Jack along with him wherever he goes, she is not helping their relationship any. In fact, she is encouraging them both to resent each other. When parents delegate such responsibilities wisely, with due respect for the needs, interests, and ages of each of their children, they can encourage a very special feeling of affection between them and even minimize jealousy. For children in the same family are not merely rivals, they are also often extremely warm and close companions who enjoy one another's company and have a lot of fun together.

Lessons in living

While age differences can be sources of squabbles and conflicts, they also provide important lessons in living. Each child, according to his age and position in the family, has rights and privileges—as well as responsibilities—which should be understood and respected. You do not allow your ten-year-old to do all the things permitted your thirteen-year-old. Nor do you give your six-year-old all the prerogatives his nine-year-old brother enjoys.

"Johnny gets to stay up until nine o'clock. Why can't I?" asks six-year-old Peter Marlin. And Mrs. Marlin gives him a definite answer, which Peter can understand and accept, even if grudgingly.

"Your brother is older, but when you get to be nine, you'll also be allowed to stay up later. You know, most of your friends have the same eight o'clock bedtime you do. But when they're older, they'll be able to stay up longer and do other more grown-up things, too."

Being specific about the fact that each age brings with it certain privileges—as well as certain obligations—helps a child know that he is being treated fairly, that he will be accorded his share of independence as he is ready for it. Waiting for the added privileges that come with added years is not easy for any child, but it is an ability you must help him develop. He will protest, but if you are fair about most things, chances are that he won't think you are against him when you have to forbid him pleasures his older brothers and sisters already enjoy. The ability to defer gratification grows slowly, but grow it must if a child is to learn right from wrong.

Some mothers and fathers expect brothers and sisters in the same family to do everything together and take an interest in the same things just because they happen to live under the same roof with the same set of parents. Brothers and sisters need to get away from each other part of the time. They need friends and interests outside the home, and separate from one another.

When Janet Stuart was planning her eighth birthday

party, her mother suggested that she include her ten-year-old brother Eddie on her invitation list. Janet was not terribly enthusiastic, but she went along with the idea.

"Well, I'm not coming," announced Eddie, when he got wind of the plans. "I'm going to the movies with Joe and Al. I hate girls, and I don't want to play those *baby* games."

"I didn't know you hated your sister," said Mrs. Stuart, teasing Eddie.

"Oh, Mom, you know I don't," Eddie answered, "but I'm not going to that silly old party."

Mrs. Stuart smiled as she realized that Eddie was, and should be, more interested in spending time with his ten-year-old buddies than he was in going to Janet's party. Why in the world, she asked herself, had she expected him to enjoy being with his sister's younger friends?

When Mrs. Stuart mentioned Eddie's behavior to her husband, he laughed and said, "When I was Eddie's age I couldn't stand my little sister's friends. I was contemptuous of *all* girls—but obviously I got over it!"

A family council

Some families find that sitting down together regularly in a kind of family council helps iron out difficulties and foster better understanding. Such sessions give everyone a chance to offer suggestions, air grievances, discuss rules, and make plans. Not all families feel comfortable doing this, and some prefer to discuss things informally whenever an issue arises, but many find it a pleasant and workable arrangement.

When parents encourage youngsters to talk over their feelings with them from the time they are little, they are even then helping them along the road to ethical behavior. For by allowing feelings to come out in the open and be examined and discussed, parents can clear up many of their children's confusions and conflicts, and thus help them develop a genuine sense of right and wrong. And when mothers and fathers accept each child for himself as he is, and give each one the opportunity to make the most of his unique capacities, they are helping them all to value themselves and to appreciate each other. They are fostering in their children those healthy qualities that underlie all ethical behavior.

Chapter seven

SELFHOOD:

℞ FOR BROTHERHOOD

The flood of violent reactions following attempts to implement the Supreme Court's decision outlawing school segregation has brought the subject of race prejudice more squarely out in the open than ever before in our recent history.

As a result, many conscientious parents in all parts of our country have been challenged to re-examine their own feelings and attitudes. They ask themselves what they as individuals can do about prejudice. They want to know how it develops and how they can guard their children from acquiring it and being affected by it. Convinced that blind hatred is not only deeply wrong but damaging as well, both to those who hate and to those who are hated, many mothers and fathers are seeking answers to help them immunize their children against the disease of bigotry.

The seeds of prejudice

Prejudice arises out of many causes: custom, conformity, fear, anger—present singly or in combination. One thing is known for certain: No child is born prejudiced. But children—very early and all on their own—learn to exclude. When little Wendy chooses Joan for her exclusive playmate and shuts out Ethel, she is doing so, not out of what we as adults know as prejudice, but out of her need to feel special and close to her friend. All too often this "need to belong" develops into a "need to look down upon" as children acquire feelings of prejudice from their parents, relatives, and friends—all of whom have acquired their feelings from *their* parents, relatives, and friends.

It has been estimated that in the United States only ten per cent of the population at the least, and twenty per cent at the most, can be said to be relatively free of prejudice. A good deal of this prejudice falls into the conforming type with its roots in the need to cling to the familiar and to fear and resent the unfamiliar. Many people express racial and religious prejudices out of this need to go along with what they consider the conventions of their group. In so doing, they seek to bolster their own feeling of belonging at the expense of excluding those representing another group.

Since these tendencies exist in greater or less degree in a large proportion of the adult population, it is not difficult to understand how they can arise almost spontaneously in children who are not yet at all certain of their status in even their own small world. It takes a great deal of strength for an adult to dissociate himself from the ideas of those whose love and esteem he needs and wants. Think of how nearly impossible it is for a child. Under ideal conditions, a child's early tendencies to conform need not become a pattern for prejudice. But since ideal conditions do not exist around us, all parents concerned with the ethical development of their children must play a continuing role to see that these tendencies do not develop into unethical and stereotyped racial or religious attitudes.

Even very young children are not unaware of racial differences. One white nursery school youngster, sitting across from a Negro child who was new to the group, turned to him and remarked, "Goodness, your mommy forgot to wash your face this morning." Having made this unemotional observation, she went right back to her finger painting.

Jerry, another child in the same neighborhood and a bright youngster, asked if he could bring a boy home for lunch. His mother was delighted that he had found a friend so soon. She was a little surprised, but not at all critical, when their guest turned out to be a Negro. Several days later she said in an offhand way to Jerry, "You never mentioned that Joe was colored." Jerry thought for a second and then said, "I guess I didn't really notice, but I'll look next time I invite somebody home—if you'll remind me to."

How prejudice grows

Early awareness of differences is for the most part simply an indication of interest and curiosity, not an evidence of incipient prejudice. Yet if a child has been taught to feel strongly that dirt is always "bad," small bebeginnings of a feeling of white superiority may be in the making. His pre-logical thinking often runs this way: "Dirt is bad. Dirt is dark. Dark is bad. Negroes are dark. Negroes are bad."

All children go through a stage of pre-logical thinking before they learn to think effectively. Moving ahead to the next step in their thinking about and evaluating those of another color will depend a great deal, as we have already pointed out, upon the attitudes and examples of their parents primarily and then upon those of their teachers and classmates.

Sometimes, as in the case of eight-year-old Connie Bryant, signs of intolerance show themselves where least expected. Connie is a happy, outgoing youngster whose parents are loving and intelligent. Imagine her mother's shock when the little girl, rushing into the house after visiting a friend, announced loudly, "I hate colored kids. Laura's mother says they all lie and steal."

Alarmed and angry at hearing this pronouncement from the lips of her own child, Mrs. Bryant's first reaction was to denounce Laura's mother to Connie for being stupid and prejudiced, and to tell her daughter how wrong such beliefs were. But she managed to restrain herself.

"I wonder where in the world Laura's mother ever got that mistaken idea," she said calmly to Connie. "Some white children lie and some white children steal, but not all of them do, and that goes for colored children, too."

After Connie went to bed, Mr. and Mrs. Bryant talked the whole matter over. They knew that while Connie valued her friendship with Laura, she valued their approval even more, and wanted very much to be like them. They decided to make their own feelings clearer to her. After all, they realized, Connie had just been parroting something she had heard away from home. As the days went by, the Bryants found appropriate opportunities to explain to Connie, in ways she could understand, what they stood for and why they did not agree with Laura's mother.

Several weeks later Mrs. Bryant overheard Connie making this careful explanation to Laura, "It's only mean kids we don't like—it doesn't matter whether they're white *or* colored."

This is not the only encounter with prejudiced thinking Connie is likely to come across, but her exposure to it was benign. When Connie repeated the generalization about Negroes made by her friend's mother, she did so out of her own lack of knowledge plus her desire to conform by agreeing. At the time she did not know any better, but now she does. Now she understands what her family—whom she wants very much to be like—believes in. They are teaching her that people are to be judged as individuals, not looked down upon as a group because they are of a different color, race, or religion. We cannot foretell the future for young Connie Bryant, but it is extremely unlikely that she will develop into a hostile, prejudiced adult. For most important of all, her parents love and respect her—and they show it. They treat her fairly and considerately and have helped her develop a healthy self-esteem.

Placing the blame on others

It is a different story with another eight-year-old, Timmy Dirks. "He has to be made to learn," his parents say when they hand out stiff punishments to him for all kinds of things, from spilling his milk to teasing the dog. Fairness and consideration have been bypassed in their zeal to "train him properly." They have blamed him so often and so indiscriminately that he has come to think of himself as a pretty low character. (See also Chapter III, *Spare the Child*, p. 44.)

Feeling unworthy, Timmy may try to escape his parents' displeasure by placing the blame on others. He may see it as a way to raise his own estimate of himself. Timmy's parents do not realize that by blaming him unfairly for *everything*, they may well be making him unable to accept blame for *anything*. And if he cannot blame himself, he may blame others, very often seeing them as more blameworthy than in truth they are.

Prejudiced adults are very often products of this kind of treatment. Secretly fearing that they themselves are evil, they turn their hatred against the evil they ascribe to others. That is why so many of them are determined to make scapegoats of members of minority groups.

Prejudice by imitation

Some children acquire their parents' prejudices, not because they have been harshly treated, but because their very love compels an unwitting imitation of their mothers' and fathers' attitudes. Take the Jerrolds, for example. They would be the first to deny that they are sowing the seeds of one form of unethical behavior—that is, prejudice—in the minds of their impressionable youngsters. Joe, Sr., is a well-known lawyer and respected citizen in his town, and his wife Marian a tireless volunteer community worker. Conscientious parents, they are proud of young Joe and his sister Sally, and try to do their very best for them. Yet every time Mr. Jerrold makes a sneering remark about people of a different race, or his wife condemns an entire group for the shortcomings of a few, they are establishing a pattern of prejudice for Joe, Jr., and Sally to follow. And the youngsters are influenced still more by how their parents act toward members of other groups in their presence. Sally cannot help catching the condescension in her mother's voice when she talks to the Negro grocery boy. Nor can Joe miss the subtle difference in the way his father treats people of another religion.

Parents who are themselves friendly and democratic teach their children to accept and appreciate the uniqueness in people. They also provide standards of fairness and decency for their youngsters to emulate. They try to give them opportunities to meet and to know others of different races and religions. Ethical behavior involves respect for the rights of others. If a child is to be helped to behave ethically, he must see that respect in action in his parents' dealings with *all* people. From their day-to-day example, their comments and practices, he learns respect for others.

Self-esteem a must

But how can a child learn to respect others if he himself has not been respected? If he has not learned to respect himself? A child who knows that his parents value him, just as he is, is free to value others. And, as we have discussed in the preceding chapter, how he has been helped to handle his rivalry with his brothers and sisters is vital to his self-acceptance. When a child feels wanted and secure, he will not have to despise others to prove his own worth, nor will he claim a superiority for himself that deep down he does not really feel.

For by no means can all prejudice be explained away by the simple need to conform. Much of it is born, not out of a need to be loved, but out of a deep need to hate. A person who is driven by the need to hate others is displaying, whether he knows it or not, how much he hates himself. For a variety of reasons he has come to think of himself as basically unworthy and unlovable. This was the case with twelve-year-old Glenn Collins.

Glenn's older sister was a very much wanted child, and more than eleven years went by before Glenn was born. The Collinses, a little embarrased at having a new baby, could never fully accept Glenn. Helen was always neat, they told him, good in school, no trouble, a pleasure to have around. Nothing Glenn did could ever compare favorably with Helen's performance. Small wonder he came to think of himself as never going to amount to much. But Glenn tried to find a way out of his secret misery. He joined three other boys in a campaign of harassment against the Negro children on the playground. Deriding them and calling them names was Glenn's way of trying to bolster his own feeble self-esteem.

If no help and understanding are provided for Glenn, the future looks bleak indeed, not only for him but for those he comes in contact with. Inner turmoil like Glenn's generally becomes more intense as time goes on. As he gets older, his prejudice may well take on an even more virulent character. Driven to justify it, he may become obsessed with the need to gather "facts" and "data" which he can then use to substantiate his intolerance and confirm his hatreds. Thus we see full-blown evil emerging, of which too many examples are in evidence today on our national scene.

Prejudice from displaced anger

Many parents, seeing newspaper and magazine pictures of white mothers protesting desegregation, were shocked at the naked and brutal anger in the faces of these women. Blind prejudice is very often a form of displaced anger, that is, a centering of anger upon something or someone other than that which originally aroused it. If parents are to teach their children right from wrong, here again they must understand how important it is to give them opportunities to express their anger in words when they *first* feel it.

The day six-year-old Rosalie Harder stamped her foot and yelled at her mother, "I hate you—you mean old thing," Mrs. Harder wasn't exactly pleased. She was tempted to say, "Go upstairs and stay there until you've learned to be polite," but wisely she did not. Besides realizing that politeness is not learned that way, Mrs. Harder knew that she must help Rosalie to let her feelings come out in words, but not in undisciplined actions. If they talked about them, perhaps she could keep her youngster from feeling overwhelmingly guilty.

"I remember the day I said that very thing to my mother," Mrs. Harder told her. "All children feel like that at times, and it does them good to talk about it. You're angry with me because I won't let you go over to Selma's this afternoon, and that's all right—I understand it. But I have a notion you don't really hate me to pieces, even though you are good and mad."

By talking about how Rosalie felt and not scolding her, Mrs. Harder made it plain that she understood and accepted her daughter's feelings. Giving a child freedom to feel anger and to talk about it is all-important if he is to learn to behave ethically. Because Rosalie was helped to put her feelings into words, she was able to come to a clearer understanding of them. If Rosalie's mother had not encouraged her to find the words to express her feelings, soon Rosalie would have no words for them. And with no words she could not think about her emotions—she would simply bury them. But they would not have disappeared. They would still be part of her—covered up, but waiting to explode against someone else.

Discuss hostile feelings openly

Every time you encourage your children to talk about their hostile feelings openly, you give them opportunities to examine and deal with them, and you help them avoid displacing those feelings on others. While the original occasion that evoked their "bad" childhood feelings will have long since disappeared, nevertheless if those feelings have been bottled up, they may well persist only to be again called up and perhaps vented on members of minority groups.

While ethical adults want to see all human beings treated and judged on the basis of their own worth, not their color, they realize that a great many people of their generation have lived their entire lives in a segregated society and have incorporated the beliefs and feelings of that society into their adult personalities. They understand that it is not

easy for many of these parents to relinquish their prejudices. But attitudes have been modified through direct
personal experiences in places of employment, parents'
meetings, churches, and elsewhere. However, many deeply
religious parents express rabid prejudices despite the in-
compatibility of their prejudice with their professed religious beliefs. This cannot help but confuse a child and do
serious damage to his ethical development. When a youngster attends church where he is told to love others as he
loves himself, he has trouble making that idea jibe with
the opposite one: that is, hate others that his parents are
prejudiced against.

When the Turners, who were highly regarded in their
community, made their own stand on segregation clear
and demonstrated their beliefs, they helped modify the
opinions of many mothers and fathers. At a parents' meeting they pointed out how inappropriate and inconsistent
narrow prejudices are in today's world.

"No matter what our old attitudes are, we do our children an injustice," Mr. Turner declared, "when we do not
encourage them to know others of different races and
cultures. How will they be able to play an effective part in
this changing world of ours if we restrict their knowledge?"

The Turners were influential in reducing prejudices
among parents because they themselves were respected
and admired members of the community, and many people
wanted to conform with the Turner's views. Also Jeff
Turner's picture of the modern world made many parents
stop to think. Practically all of them were concerned with
having their children learn more and know more than they
did.

Attitudes can change

More and more children are being exposed to integra-
tion and will continue to be. They will experience situa-

tions completely different from any that their parents encountered when they were young. And because most parents do not want to block their children's opportunity to obtain an education, there is hope that the worst result of prejudice—namely, outright discrimination—will eventually be done away with. The aim of anti-discrimination laws is not to reduce prejudice, but to control its overt expression, to give equal opportunities to all. When the overt expression of prejudice in the form of outright discrimination changes, very often ideas about prejudice change, too, although slowly. Anti-discrimination laws not only can create an atmosphere that discourages the development of prejudice, but they may well produce situations in which existing prejudices can eventually be eradicated.

Parenthood, as you well know, does not automatically change a person's irrational beliefs. However, parents' meetings in desegregated schools, for example, bring all parents together for the good of their children. There, out of a common bond—their children—they can learn to work together co-operatively. And when white parents come to know Negro parents, they learn that they face many of the same child-rearing problems and have the same pride and concern for their young. Now that many white parents are seeing Negro parents for the first time as human beings, not as stereotypes, they are beginning to change their old attitudes.

Although not so rapidly as many people would like, a good deal of progress is being made in the reduction of prejudiced belief as well as prejudiced behavior. Many churches, labor unions, schools, and civic groups are working tirelessly in a variety of different ways to achieve these goals. It would be naïve to assume that bigotry will disappear easily or completely. But since blind hatred is clearly an evil, every parent concerned with the ethical development of his child will guard against sowing a single seed of intolerance. As we have pointed out throughout this book, parents are the child's early models of ethical behavior. But children are bound to be confused about right and wrong if the sum total of a parent's words and actions seems to imply, "Do as I say, not as I do." Just as a child is not born "good," neither is he born with prejudice. In the truly ethical person there is no room for blind hatred.

Chapter eight

THERE IS NOTHING

LIKE A DAD!

Fathers seem to be coming in for more than their rightful share of criticism these days. Those undifferentiated and carping attacks on mothers that gave us the word "momism" have now given way to what may soon be termed "dadism." When a young father regularly takes a hand at giving his baby a bath or changing his diaper, there is sure to be a critic lurking behind the scenes somewhere to warn him that he is in danger of losing his masculinity. "How will his child ever know what a man's role in life really is," asks the viewer-with-alarm, "if father performs these womanly chores?"

Changes in "masculine" and "feminine" roles

Our society has witnessed tremendous changes in the roles traditionally assigned to men and women. Today there is a great overlapping in what used to be considered strictly mother's or father's province. For the most part, modern parents accept without question their joint responsibility for sharing the duties (as well as the joys) of child care. Practically no one nowadays believes that taking care of a baby is entirely a mother's job. There is general agreement that while fathers and mothers are equally important to their children, they are important in different ways.

Obviously, a new baby is much closer to his mother than to his father because he is so dependent on her. And while fathers are not expected to give as many bottles or change as many diapers as mothers do, more and more of them are taking over some of the baby's physical care. They find it not only comfortable, but possible, to be helpful fathers and real men at the same time. Nor do they seem to be creating so much confusion about their respective roles that their child runs the risk of being unable to tell the players without a scorecard. A man who does not feel it unmanly to bathe a baby is not in danger of blurring for his youngster the picture of what it takes to be a man. The child's image of his father as strong and masculine is not likely to disappear down the drain with the bath water.

Take the plunge, Daddy-O

Some young fathers feel bashful and "all thumbs" when it comes to taking care of a new baby, even though they might like to give it a whirl now and then. If that is the way you feel, it is a good idea to try your hand, anyway. Once you take the plunge, it becomes easier. More than that, you feel closer to your baby right from the start. Sometimes it becomes harder later on, especially as you see his mother becoming more and more expert at handling him.

Perhaps you belong to that sizable group of fathers who feel something less than enchantment at the notion of bathing a baby or changing his diaper. For some men fatherhood often takes a little growing into. Even if you do not take on any of the baby's physical care, you perform one important function as a new father when you give your wife needed moral support. By helping her feel happy and adequate as a woman and a mother, you are also contributing vitally to your baby's well-being. You provide him with a mother who feels more certain of herself because she has your assurance that she is doing a good job.

Joel Carton admits he never felt like a "real father" until young Joel was about seven months old. His pride knew no bounds when the baby started looking toward the door each evening when he was told it was time for Daddy to come home. "From then on, being a father was marvelous," he admits, "and it got better every day." Babies around young Joel's age enjoy playing with their fathers, and show it. Peekaboo or pat-a-cake with Daddy are endless sources of delight—for baby, at any rate.

Here is where your patience can stand testing. The nineteenth pat-a-cake may bore you, but not your young one. Of course, you will not go on and on, but stopping abruptly is like snatching an object away from the baby without replacing it with something else. A baby's attention can easily be diverted, and going along with his simple joys for a reasonable time can make your relationship warmer. These games will not interest him forever. Meanwhile you will have laid the groundwork for sharing the more "sophisticated" interests that will develop as he grows older.

Fathers, the key to the outside world

Your children learn from you how men are supposed to act. Your son gets to know from your example what men are like and what is expected of them. He learns to be manly because he has you as a model to pattern himself after. When your three-year-old sits in your armchair and pretends to smoke a pipe the way you do, he is showing how much he wants to be like you.

Later on, even if his mother also works, your son learns that a responsible father is expected to protect and care for his wife and children. You represent his most important first link to the outside world. He learns a great deal even when he simply overhears your "man talk" about events in the office or shop, your comments on the day's news, your chat with another fellow. He thinks of you as a "strong guy" even if you do not. "My father can lick your father" is more than an idle boast!

Your daughter, too, acquires an ingredient essential to her ethical development—self-confidence—from your love and approval and your wholehearted acceptance of her as she is. The kind of relationship she enjoys with you will affect her friendship with boys and other men. From you she forms a concept of the man she can love and respect, the man she will eventually marry.

All through their childhood your sons and daughters continue to learn about maleness from you. They learn about right and wrong, about the outside world, about responsibility, as they absorb your attitudes and observe your actions. Your importance to their ethical development cannot be overestimated.

Phil Kerwin is the idol of his four-year-old daughter, Barbara. He cannot possibly do a single thing she does not admire. From her point of view, the only person marring the bliss in the Kerwin household is that boarder (her name is Mom) whom Barbara would love to evict. "Daddy, why don't you and I go to the country all by ourselves next weekend?" Barbara asks her father. "Mom can come out one day and cook for us."

Barbara's father is flattered by this adoration—he would be the first to admit it. But he knows how important it is to help Barbara come to realize that she cannot win out in this small-scale triangle. And she needs help, too, in feeling comfortable about her excessive devotion to her father at the expense of her mother. Recognizing this, he often comes up with this kind of plan: "You and I are going to the park Saturday afternoon, Babs, but on Sunday it's Mom's turn. Then I am taking her to a concert."

He keeps Barbara from resenting her mother by accepting his daughter's devotion, but not overstressing it. He also lets her know that while most little girls love their fathers best for a while, they will not always and forever. By showing a friendly concern for a daughter's interests and activities but not making too much of her love for him, a father helps her relinquish her competition with her mother and pattern herself after her, which she wants very much to do. Through satisfying relationships with both parents, a daughter can learn to choose her own husband when the time comes, and to form a warm and loving relationship with him and with the children they will someday have.

Boys can be jealous of their dads

But fathers are often not nearly as amused or as understanding when their young sons want to shut *them* out. Despite his love and admiration for his father, four-year-old Ned is jealous of him, and Sam Cooke is not always happy about it. Practically all young boys want to share in the special attentions their mothers give their fathers, which they are well aware are not for them. By the time children have reached Ned's age, they know and resent the fact that their parents occupy a room together where they are not always welcome, that mother and father go out together and like to be alone, and that they even take an occasional trip by themselves, without including their young ones.

Ned's father used to get annoyed at him and call him a "mamma's boy" for demanding so much of his mother's attention and wanting to be with her just as much as his sister was. But as Sam Cooke realized that Ned had to be helped to give up this rivalry with him, as well as to cope with his envy of his sister, he learned how to handle the situation better. He overlooked Ned's occasional sulkiness, which diminished somewhat as the two of them spent more time together in some strictly male pursuits.

Sam Cooke could afford to be generous to his rival. After all, little Ned could not possibly emerge victorious from this contest. But he also realized the importance of presenting Ned with a picture of a manly man—one who was a loving husband as well as a loving father. A frequent "Say, Ned, look after Mom while I am away. I have to work late at the office" gave the youngster permission to take his father's place while he was not at home. But it did not allow Ned to have his mother all to himself. That would only have made him feel frightened and guilty. Gradually, as all boys must, Ned learned that he could not win. It was almost as if his thoughts ran this way: "You have to be a man to get a woman. I'll copy Dad. That's how he got Mom. When I get bigger and more like him, I'll get someone like her myself."

Both you and your wife ease your youngsters through this stage of their development by making it clear that each of you is already spoken for. That while your daughter cannot have you to herself or your son have his mother to himself, neither one of you is shocked at their bid for your exclusive attention. The growth of ethical behavior, based as it is on deep feelings of love and sympathy, justice and fairness, courage and loyalty, has its beginnings way back in these early struggles. Here patterns for future relationships of all kinds get their start. The acceptance of one's

127

capabilities and one's limitations, the ability to wait, the appreciation of, and need for, others—all have their roots in these early years. But by the time your youngsters are around six, they will realize that they cannot have parents all to themselves and will stop trying. When things have been handled reasonably well (no one manages this perfectly!), their interests can now turn away from you and go out to include school, their teachers, and their friends.

The rise of daddy's star

Many fathers feel that they come into their own at last when their children are in school. Now they can really talk to them and begin to reason with them. As these youngsters grow and learn more, you have many opportunities to share your views with them on many ethical questions. You make further contributions to their development when you give them new experiences and expose them to new ideas as they are ready for them.

To your grade-school child you stand more clearly than ever for protection. When ten-year-old George gets into mischief and says to his sister, "Don't tell. I'll catch it if Daddy finds out," he is showing how much he relies on his father to make him stop misbehaving, even if he cannot himself. When you do not stop your youngster from doing what he knows he should not do, the enormity of being solely responsible for his actions may actually overwhelm him. He may even mislay the sense of right and wrong he has been gradually building up over the years. This does not mean that you set up harsh, inflexible rules or demand instant obedience. You already know that such tactics do not make for good family relationships, that they are no guarantee of ethical behavior. If you are overstrict, you run the risk of rearing a child who must always look for an absolute authority to let him know what he must and must not do. He might well become the kind of adult who can never make up his mind, never know what is right—let alone stand up for it.

Be firm—and friendly

Murray Fisher's father is not firm enough with him. He explains it this way, "I was always afraid of my father because he was so tough on me when I was a boy. I don't want Murray to feel the same way about me." Wanting at all costs to avoid having his son resent him as he resented his father, Mr. Fisher rarely shows anger when Murray displeases him. He leaves what disciplining there is to his wife. This makes it difficult for her, and it is hard on Murray, who feels uncertain most of the time. He knows when he has done something wrong, and he wants his father to correct him. When Mr. Fisher says nothing, Murray gets more frightened, not less so. He feels that his father's displeasure must be piling up somewhere, just waiting to explode. He is constantly afraid of what will happen if it ever does. Clearly Mr. Fisher is defeating his purpose. He is giving Murray no notion of how firm a fair and loving father can be, and unfortunately he is encouraging that very fear and resentment he set out to avoid.

A firm and friendly attitude is a father's best bet. While you do not set impossible standards, you never hesitate to make it clear that not everything goes. Talking about your own mistakes when you were a boy is an honest and helpful thing to do. When your son realizes that you grew up to be a strong and responsible father even though you were often foolish at his age, then he knows that he stands a good chance of making it, too. And girls, just as much as boys, need fathers who set sensible limits and uphold reasonable standards. More than that, both sons and daughters need to know that their fathers like them and approve of them just as they are—fast or slow, boys or girls, quiet or lively, handsome or plain.

Fred Thomson is a busy man *and* a good father. While he would like to spend more time with his family than he can these days, he has resisted feeling guilty about it. Realizing that his youngsters had no clear picture of what he did all day and how he earned his living, Mr. Thomson invited nine-year-old Alice and seven-year-old Bud into town for lunch and a visit to the office. Seeing where their father went every day and talking with him about his work not only made the youngsters feel important and closer to him, it gave them some firsthand knowledge of what kept him so busy, why he sometimes came home too bushed for more than a quick hug. That office visit (due for a repeat performance soon) and the many quiet talks with their father that followed gave them a clearer picture of his role in the outside world. Fred Thomson's children never have the feeling he is not interested in them despite his infrequent PTA attendance. He spends lots of time with them when he can, and when he cannot, they understand why.

Negative examples have their uses too

The importance of your example has already been pointed out. Even a negative example sometimes has its points. The Langley family had planned to drive to the country for dinner on Sunday. But when Sunday came and a heavy snowfall with it, Dad had to admit he had forgotten to order the snow tires he had promised he would. As a result, the outing had to be canceled. While the youngsters were disappointed, they realized that even their own father could slip up on occasion and neglect his obligations. Mr. Langley's frank and good-humored apology helped his children feel less helpless—and far less hopeless—about their own lapses. His usual reliability was a continuing source of strength and confidence to the Langley children.

As your school-age children take on more and more responsibilities, they often need your guidance in managing conflicting ones. Frank Smith is the "Voice of Reason" in his house, and the family likes it that way. Here are some typical problems that can come up any evening in the Smith household. Chuck is supposed to clean up the cellar this Saturday, but his team has called an extra practice session. Margaret has promised to take care of her little sister, but her girl friend wants her to come over and help her with an algebra problem. Mark is sitting down to his homework when he gets an SOS from his pal, Billy, to rush over and help him fix his bicycle.

Frank Smith and his youngsters talk these things over, weigh the pros and cons together, and try to decide on what takes priority. In his role as friendly arbitrator, Father makes several suggestions. Maybe Chuck can get up early and get most of the cellar done, if not all of it, before he has to join his teammates. Maybe Margaret's friend can come to *her* house for help with her algebra. Or perhaps she'll just have to wait for another day. And Mark must finish his homework before he can help Billy fix the bike. While fathers want their youngsters to feel responsible to others, they must also point out which responsibilities must be met first. When you do not undervalue what your children consider important, you enable them to weigh one alternative against another and come to a responsible decision.

Too much responsibility

Once in a while a father insists on a son's taking on too much responsibility. Nine-year-old Allen, for example, had been begging for a dog for almost a year. When his father gave him one for Christmas, he laid down the law. "The responsibility for Trixie is all yours, Allen," he told him. "You're old enough now to be in complete charge of her."

Allen was devoted to Trixie and took faithful care of her. But on the rare occasions when he does not get home at Trixie's feeding time, his sister is not allowed to fill the dog's dish because his father had pronounced Trixie "Allen's responsibility." Mutual helpfulness is an important element in ethical behavior, but no one demonstrates it to Allen, at least where Trixie is concerned. An occasional assist would make him no less responsible for the care of his dog. Allen's father was plainly being too hard on him. (Not to mention poor Trixie!)

When youngsters (daughters, especially) move into their teens, fathers sometimes feel left out. The evening fifteen-year-old Karen Jaffy, looking almost grown-up in her first long dress, waited anxiously in the living room for her escort, her father had to admit to himself that he felt suddenly deposed and even a mite jealous. He knew that from now on Karen would be more and more interested in boys—less and less in him. Still it came as something of a shock—now he was "the older generation."

Wondering where the time had flown, Mr. Jaffy knew that he would have to co-operate with the inevitable. And of course he did, even though he had an occasional twinge of well-concealed jealousy. For many years now he and his wife had shared their beliefs and standards with Karen. She knew what they stood for, and what they expected of her. And because she had grown up in a home where she was loved and valued, she possessed a large measure of self-confidence and self-respect. These qualities would help her develop satisfactory relationships with boys and would guide her behavior, even though she would experience the normal ups and downs as she grew to maturity. Sometimes, without even being aware of it, a girl tries to escape from her excessive attachment to her father by indulging in

132

blindly-driven entanglements with a number of boys. Luckily, this would not be so for Karen.

The look-alike crowd

Russ Kahn worries about the amount of time his fifteen-year-old son, Phil, spends with his crowd now that he is in high school. "It is not really the time so much," he explains, "but the fact that they act and even think so much alike. I can hardly pick out my own son from all the rest."

Mr. Kahn is underestimating the crowd's importance for Phil. Phil and his friends bolster each other, get a lot of gripes off their chest, and try to work out many of their doubts and uncertainties when they get together. Phil knows that his friends are not so likely to be as critical of his shortcomings as his father might be. After all, he and his pals are all in the same boat. This acting alike and sounding alike are necessary right now for Phil and his friends. They represent an identification with their own generation that is part of growing up. Phil is on his way to becoming a solid citizen, and Mr. Kahn need not fear that he will never have a personality all his own. Phil has many special and distinct qualities, and he is getting ready to move ahead and gain recognition for himself as an individual, not just as part of a group.

Sometimes parents need to band together for their own "protection" and to look into their youngsters' insistence that "everybody else in the crowd is allowed to." When Fred King's fifteen-year-old son told him that all the boys he knew were allowed to practice driving their father's cars on Sunday mornings, he couldn't quite believe it. After all, none of the boys was legally permitted to practice driving alone. When Mr. King asked a few other fathers, the story turned out to be that *one* boy, who already had his learner's permit, was driving on Sunday mornings. None of the other boys was willing to admit that his father objected,

133

and each gave out the notion that it would probably be O.K. But when Mr. King decided to investigate, the whole story fell apart.

A father's problems

Often a father's own problems stand in the way of helping his teen-ager with his. That does not mean that you have to be "problemless" to help your youngster become an ethically mature adult. It does mean, however, that a father who can look at his own problems frankly and courageously and who makes constructive efforts to solve them will be in a better position to understand any difficulties his youngster may be having. And also better able to offer guidance when it is needed.

Try not to be discouraged if you do not always understand all the reasons behind your teen-ager's varied behavior. He does not understand them all himself. You need not feel that you have failed as a father when things seem too much for you or your youngster does not want to talk. Practically all teen-agers, no matter how warm and good their relationship with their family, find it difficult at times to confide in either of their parents. They often need an adult friend outside the family with whom they can talk freely.

Understanding this, you can make it possible for your youngster to confide in another without any sense of disloyalty to you. He cannot complain to you about his mother, or to his mother about you, without feeling disloyal. Right now he is so filled with mixed emotions about his parents that he feels freer and does better when he can discuss his problems with an outsider.

Fathers are necessary

From infancy through adolescence children need fathers to help them develop soundly and to teach them right from wrong. Naturally, the demands of fatherhood shift and change as your children grow, but on one point there is no disagreement: Fathers are every bit as essential as mothers in the lives of their sons and daughters. And because they are men they have their own very special and important ways of helping their boys and girls grow up to become mature, ethical adults.

Chapter nine

BUY-BUY BABY

"Mommy, I've just got to have that new walking, talking doll," announces eight-year-old Kathy, rushing into the house at top speed. "Mary has one. You know, we saw it on TV. And it's wonderful. I really *need* it. Please!"

"Take it easy, Kathy," her mother answers. "You have so many dolls, and besides that one costs twelve dollars."

"Oh, Mom, can't you just charge it? Or ask Daddy to write a check?"

Next door, Johnny Roberts, who is six, badgers his mother constantly to stock up on more and more cereal, although the kitchen cabinet is already bulging with every known kind. But Johnny simply has to have those prizes inside the boxes, and he needs those box tops which promise even greater treasures—all of which are dangled before him daily.

Seven-year-old Allen Stuart is after his parents to buy him an expensive new robot spaceman who can (it says here in the ad) do almost everything except travel to the moon. But Allen already has a closetful of toys and gadgets that he no longer plays with. His parents can afford to buy him the spaceman, but they are beginning to wonder where all this acquisitiveness is leading to, and whether they should not, at some point soon, draw the line.

Gimme-itis

These familiar scenes are repeated all over America to-day. Children, as well as their parents, are bombarded on all sides with constant exhortations to buy, buy, buy. It doesn't even matter if you don't have the money, you can pay for it another day. Possessions of all kinds seem to arrive on the buy-now-pay-someday plan. And enough is *never* enough—there is always something new to be added.

Is it any wonder that so many youngsters suffer from chronic gimme-itis? Parents do like to buy things for their children and enjoy making them happy. But what about this constant "I-need-it" refrain? Do children really need all the things they say they do? Must they have what all the other kids have?

It is about time parents took a firm stand to counteract the blatant commercialism directed at their children. While the young know that money does not grow on trees, they could stand a bit of reminding that it does not come from credit cards or charge accounts either, and that checks are only as good as the money in the family bank account. Many parents are at a loss as to how to teach their young-sters the relationship of money to all those possessions they are "supposed" to have, and to give them some understand-ing of the work and responsibility it takes to provide the necessities as well as the luxuries and "extras." Just telling them about it can sound like complaining. They learn best when they can actually earn money themselves. Later on in this chapter we shall discuss more fully the importance of appropriate paid jobs for youngsters.

Values that get cloudy

In today's world where material possessions are increasingly important to so many people, and where there is so much to buy, a clear-cut sense of values sometimes gets cloudy. Your own values will, of course, influence your children's values, as well as their use of money and their attitudes toward it. While you want them to learn to use and manage money wisely, you also want them to develop attitudes about it in relation to other things in life on which there are no price tags. Children must learn about the intangibles which money cannot buy, in addition to those tangibles it can. You have the right and the responsibility to let your children know where you stand: "This is how *we* do it. This is what *we* believe. These are the things *we* think are important. We don't necessarily have to have the same things as the Jeffersons next door, or the Appletons up the street."

The pressures to conform—to be like the neighbors and to have what they have—are intense these days. In their own lives parents can demonstrate to their children that they are not afraid to be themselves, to have their own values, and to stick by them.

The importance of an allowance

Most parents today take it for granted that their children should begin to get an allowance when they are about six or seven, and many recognize the value of paying for specific chores in addition to an allowance. There is fairly general agreement that a child needs a small amount of money to call his own and to spend as he chooses. With

138

a no-strings-attached allowance Bobby or Susie can select among a few inexpensive items and have the fun of paying for them themselves. A child who has to wheedle money here and there from parents or grandparents may have a hard time thinking he is worth anything, especially when his friends receive a regular allowance as their due. And he may find it difficult later on to learn to manage money. Instead, he may just be learning to "manage" his elders in order to get them to loosen up their pocketbooks. Or he may take to pilfering now and then from his mother's purse.

Some parents find it difficult to give an allowance as freely and as matter-of-factly as they dish out the orange juice and the vitamins. Mrs. Duncan, for example, gives her eight-year-old daughter Betty fifty cents a week. But somehow she always "forgets" to give it until Betty has asked for it several times. Instead of giving it on Friday, which is payday and shopping day, it generally slips her mind until Saturday or Sunday. A child stands a much better chance of developing a wholesome attitude about money and about himself when his allowance is given ungrudgingly as his rightful share in the family income. When it is doled out reluctantly or treated as an indulgence, it loses its purpose.

A few parents still hand out an allowance as a reward for good behavior, or withhold it as a punishment for misbehavior. Phil Evans, for example, agreed to give his ten-year-old Tim seventy-five cents a week. But Tim knows that he has to toe the line or his allowance will be cut off. This is tantamount to having no allowance at all, for Tim is never quite certain that he will actually get it. Mr. Evans uses the purse strings in an attempt to manipulate Timmy's conduct—he pays him when he is good, and fines him when he is bad. Because there is a price tag on his behavior, Tim is learning that money can be used as a weapon, that people are "good," if they get paid for it. While Timmy may co-operate in order to get his allowance, he is not learning about right and wrong as a matter of personal responsibility. He is finding out how money can be used as a bargaining agent to gain favors or to manipulate people. At the moment, Timmy wonders just how much he can afford—to get away with.

In the Barrett family, the allowance scale troubled seven-year-old Joe who was the youngest and received thirty-five cents a week. His ten-year-old brother Donald got seventy-five cents, and Mary, age fifteen, was given quite a bit more—enough to cover her school supplies, clothing, and incidentals. Joe complained every now and then about being unfairly treated. "Why don't I get as much as Donald?" he asked his father. "I need more money, too. Don always gets the best of everything."

Mr. Barrett was patient with Joe: "When Don was your age, he got thirty-five cents, just the way you do. Next year you will get more, and when you're ten, your share will be at least as much as your brother's because you will need more money then. The amount of money I give each of you has nothing at all to do with playing favorites. Come now, Joe, I think you really know that."

Joe accepted this reasonable explanation, although it by no means erased the envy he felt for his older brother. But he was learning to wait, and in the meantime he understands that his father is playing fair with the whole bunch.

"Swiping"

Mrs. Thornton was shocked to discover that seven-year-old Dan, a perfectly happy youngster with an adequate allowance, had been going on regular "swiping" sprees at the local supermarket with his boy friend, Hal Goodman.

Before talking to the boys she decided to talk it over with Mrs. Goodman. Hal's mother was not pleased at the boys' escapades but she laughed it off: "There weren't so many supermarkets in my day, but I remember stealing from the dime store when I was their age. It is not really a major crime."

Mrs. Thornton did not consider it a major crime, either, and she did not plan a major punishment. But, she reasoned, how does any child develop an ethical attitude toward "swiping" that will deter him from stealing if his parents do not make their own attitudes clear and express their disapproval.

"Stealing is wrong, no matter what," she told Dan, "and I do not want you to do it, even if you just wanted to see if you could get away with it, or because somebody else did it. Dad and I are disappointed in you."

Dan had to agree. There was no doubt in his mind where his family stood on the issue. He knew that he had let his parents down this time, but he also felt reasonably certain that he could resist going along with such a prank again, even if Hal called him "chicken."

Buying friends

Sometimes a youngster, unsure of his worth, or in a new and difficult situation, may attempt to use the purchasing power of money to purchase some attention. Nine-year-old Steve Rogers felt lonely and out of things in the new neighborhood his family had just moved into. Steve started spending all of his allowance, and even some of his extra "chore money," treating his schoolmates to ice cream and cokes. When he ran out, he tried to get his parents to give him an advance. Mr. and Mrs. Rogers began to wonder why Steve needed so much money. "I need it for my new friends," Steve told them frankly. "I like to treat them." His father knew that Steve had not been so magnanimous with the kids in his old neighborhood where he felt more at home and at ease. "It's good of you to be so generous, Stevie," Mr. Rogers told his son. "But you don't *always* have to do the treating. How about the other kids once in a while?"

Steve's mother and father realized that he needed help to make friends in other ways. Mrs. Rogers encouraged him to bring a schoolmate home for dinner now and then, and Mr. Rogers took Steve and a couple of the boys he especially liked to a few ball games. With a little assist from his parents, Steve began to make friends. Before long he knew he could keep them, too, without bribery.

It's a different story with a five- or six-year-old who may give money away, or frequently treat his friends to bubble gum or ice pops in a sweeping gesture of generosity. When Jenny was three, Mrs. Martin despaired of her ever learning to share anything, and she tried hard to persuade her to, but Jenny was much too young then. Now Mrs. Martin is surprised and pleased that Jenny, at six, enjoys being generous. She not only wants her friends to come to the house for cookies and milk, she frequently buys them ice pops, and they do the same for her. This is all part of their budding sociability, and their expansive feelings toward one another.

Saving money

Becky Hawthorne's mother was worried about her daughter's apparent inability to put a few cents away and make her allowance last at least a week. Becky, at nine, usually took her weekly forty cents and plunked it all down at the local dime store.

"I think she ought to realize," Mrs. Hawthorne told her husband, "that while an allowance is for spending, saving a little is important, too. How will she ever learn to think of tomorrow? Isn't that part of the purpose of an allowance—to help children think and plan ahead?"

The Hawthornes decided to help their daughter by suggesting that she spend thirty or thirty-five cents, if that was what she wanted to do, and put a nickle or a dime in her piggy bank. Becky took the suggestion good-naturedly, and as a result, she had a little extra money to spend when she wanted something that cost more than her weekly allowance.

Part of the growing up process involves this ability to defer gratification. Five- and six-year-olds cannot be expected to look ahead. They live for today, not for tomorrow. But by the time they are around Becky's age, they can begin to plan ahead.

Saving to buy something—saving for a special purpose—does teach children the value of money and helps them develop the ability not only to plan ahead, but to postpone getting something they want.

Twelve-year-old Mark Clifford wanted very much to buy a pair of skis and ski boots which his father could not, at the moment, afford. Mr. Clifford talked it over with his son and told him that he would help him to save up for it. He made it possible for Mark to earn extra money by having him help clean the basement and the garage and do a few other odd jobs around the house. Mark also ran errands for the neighbors, for which he was paid. By putting away his earnings and part of his allowance, he managed to save about half of what he needed for his ski equipment, and his father contributed the balance. Mark discovered that it was quite possible to plan ahead, to save and wait for something he wanted. He also learned a good deal about the work and effort it took to accumulate money for a big purchase. And his father's stock, already high in Mark's eyes, jumped another ten points.

Attitudes towards money are imitated

The way in which parents handle their finances is naturally reflected in a child's attitude toward money. Bob and Alice Burton, for example, plan the expenditures and savings together. Bob does the banking and has specific bills to take care of, such as the mortgage, the car and insurance payments. His wife handles the bills which have to do with the running of the house. Both have a no-strings-attached allowance to spend as they please, as does their twelve-year-old daughter, Barbara.

Barbara sometimes asks to sit in on the money-management discussions to help her understand what the family's money is used for. As in almost every family, unexpected expenses throw their money-management system out of kilter. And sometimes there just doesn't seem to be enough to go around. Mr. Burton occasionally spends more than he intends to and has to dip into funds set aside for other purposes. Barbara sometimes spends all her allowance and her baby-sitting money before payday. Or she needs a new party dress just at a time when important bills are due. Because the Burtons feel free to talk about family finances with Barbara, she is helped to an understanding of what it takes to meet everyone's needs. Their honest, forthright discussions about what they can and cannot afford let her know what is reasonable to ask for and when economies are in order.

Since every family is different, the attitudes toward, as well as the management of, money will naturally differ from family to family. And brothers and sisters in the same family differ in their ability to manage money and in their feelings about it. Sally Brown, at twelve, enjoys spending her allowance as soon as she gets it. Her fourteen-year-old brother, Joseph, is careful about his money and enjoys seeing how far he can stretch a dollar. Partly this is because, in addition to his allowance, Joseph earns cash by mowing lawns, raking leaves, or shoveling snow for the neighbors. He places more value on the money that he has to work for than on the money that is given to him. But there is another reason. Joe is a whiz at arithmetic. He can figure his finances as capably and quickly as he solves his math problems at school.

The Browns take these individual differences into consideration. They do not berate Sally for being freer with her spending. Instead they try to help her plan ahead so that she will not always be short at the end of the week. The Browns know that children can and do learn from their mistakes in using money, and they realize, too, that spending habits change as children grow older and gain experience.

Youngsters like financial independence

Youngsters, past their early dependent days, do not always find it comfortable to accept steady handouts from the adults in their lives. No matter how substantial an allowance is given, nor how abundant the material goods the family can provide, being dependent on parents for everything can have a way of subtly undermining a young person's self-esteem. A youngster who is bent on asserting his independence finds it pretty hard to show gratitude for all the money and goods which come his way, even though he might like to be able to pay his own way, or earn at least part of his spending money. Opportunities to earn extra cash by working at suitable jobs—either at home, or for an older child, away from home—give a youngster an understanding of the money-value in work and a feeling of his own worth as well. For young teen-agers, working at jobs outside the home provides them with even more realistic experiences that can pave the way for greater responsibility in the future.

In an earlier era the question of whether a child should do some useful work never came up. Years ago the services of all the youngsters in the family were required. Each child, whether he lived on a farm or in the city, had specific responsibilities that had to be met for the good of all. The co-operation of everyone was needed just to keep the household running smoothly, and jobs of all kinds were the rule, not the exception. For the most part, today's families no longer live in isolated dwellings with lots of tasks for all to do, and they have not lived that way for some time. Factory-made goods, labor-saving devices, and firms offering all kinds of specialized services perform many of the chores that used to fall to the family members—young and old alike.

Useful work for children

This is no plea, even were it possible, for a return to the old days of back-breaking toil and few work-saving conveniences, the era when youngsters were kept out of school to work in the kitchen or in the fields or in the factories. Today's parents are as proud of the technical advances that have freed them from so much arduous labor as they are of their modern views on child care. They know that work in and of itself does not contain some kind of magic character-building quality. It neither automatically produces responsibility nor teaches a child right from wrong. But useful work that is appropriate and not overdemanding offers youngsters a unique sense of partnership in the family, a tangible confirmation of their personal worth, and a realistic view of what it takes to supply their needs.

The Wilson family puts this idea of useful, paid work into practice. Although they recognize that children should learn to contribute work without being paid for it, as a necessary part of family living (See Chapter VI, *Those Scene-Stealing Siblings*, p. 94), they also believe that their children should be paid for some chores, and that this source of income should be quite separate from their allowances.

Seven-year-old Barbara Wilson is expected to keep her room reasonably tidy. Her eleven-year-old sister, Ellen, sets the table and dries the dishes most nights. Both girls help their mother with some of the general housekeeping. Their brother, Wallace, who is fourteen, takes out the rubbish, keeps the yard neat, and assists his father with all sorts of minor repair jobs. These are their regular no-pay responsibilities as family members. But the two older Wilson youngsters earn extra money by doing special chores like washing windows, cleaning the basement or attic, scrubbing woodwork. This family work plan not only adds extra money to their pocketbooks, it adds inches to their stature. Later on, they expect to be able to earn money by working away from home. Next year Ellen intends to baby-sit for the neighbors, turning over one of her paid home chores to Barbara, and Wallace is already drumming up a few odd jobs—mowing lawns and running errands.

Some parents are against paying their youngsters for doing any work around the house since they already give them an allowance. The Marshalls feel that they do enough by providing good food, a decent home and clothing, not to mention toys and luxuries. "I don't see why we should also pay the kids for contributing their work," says Mr. Marshall. "We think they should learn to accept responsibility for doing things for, and with the family, *without* being paid for it."

Recognizing that their two boys, aged twelve and fourteen, need opportunities to learn more about actually earning money, the Marshalls have worked out a solution with their neighbors. The Logans, next door, always want odd jobs done and are willing to pay the Marshall boys for them. This gives the boys a chance to earn money away from home, and still contribute their work as part of their family responsibilities. Whether a youngster earns at home, away from home, or both, he learns to value himself and his services, to understand that there is money-value in work, and to take responsibility.

Wage scales for youngsters

How much should be paid for special jobs around the house? This, of course, is up to parents—what they consider the job is worth and what they can afford. When it comes to paying teen-agers, parents often get together and establish agreed-upon rates for jobs, such as baby-sitting or car-washing or snow-shoveling, which call for decent remuneration. When young people are paid fairly for a job well done, they not only learn to put effort and enthusiasm into their work, they gain personal satisfaction as well.

Adolescents frequently complain that they just do not have enough money for all the things they require and all the expenses they have. Harry Drake, at fifteen, is forever after his father for money. "My allowance is not enough, Dad," he complains. "How can I take a girl to the movies and still have money left for lunch and school stuff?" Mr. Drake thinks his son's demands are unreasonable. "I'm not *made* of money," he says. "When I was a kid, I couldn't go to my father for money. I had to earn every cent I got, or I just plain didn't have any."

"I know, Dad," argues Harry, "but this is *today*, not when you were a kid. Money doesn't go as far nowadays. Besides, with all my homework and band practice I can't find time to earn a heck of a lot."

Harry's viewpoint deserves consideration, but so does his father's. There is a limit to how much Mr. Drake can give him, and Harry needs to understand this. Perhaps he could stand more help in budgeting his allowance and in finding a job that does not take up too much time. Young people of today are under many pressures. They have to budget their time very carefully if they are to keep up with their studies, get their homework done, and still manage extra-curricular activities. For some, this means that they cannot easily manage to hold down a part-time job even when they can find one. But for those who can, there are simply not enough part-time or summer job opportunities in most communities. This problem must be faced by parents, teachers, and community leaders alike, and some kind of satisfactory solution found. In the simpler society of our grandfather's day, the family alone could be relied upon to provide work experiences for youngsters. Today more organized efforts to supply after-school and vacation work must be made by home, school, and community if youngsters are to develop constructive attitudes toward work, money, and their own worth.

The real values

As in everything else, your own standards and values will influence your youngsters' standards and values. As you get across to your children what you believe in, you are letting them know that while money is important, it is not all-important. Friendship, love, honesty, and decency toward our fellow human beings, in short, the qualities that make up ethical behavior, are still the real values in life.

Chapter ten

CONSPIRACY OF SILENCE

Inevitably a crisis of some magnitude will enter the life
of every child. If not in his own family, then in the family
of friends or neighbors, he will one day come up against
the reality of serious illness, death, separation or divorce.
Obviously, if a crisis occurs in his immediate family, the
impact on a child is greater. But even when it strikes someone he knows, he may still worry and wonder: How did
it happen? Why? Will it happen to us? Sometimes a child

is able to voice his fears and confusions. Very often he cannot.

Silence does not mean content

Many parents feel that they should shield their children for as long as they can from any and all unpleasant realities. Some evade issues completely. Others fabricate stories or give misleading answers. Still others, relieved that their children ask no questions, tell them nothing, assuming that what their youngster does not ask about has no effect upon him. Often they mistake a child's silence for peace of mind.

No conscientious parent wants to burden a child with details of illness or misfortune he cannot yet comprehend, but a simple explanation, adapted to a youngster's age and ability to understand, is his due. When a parent enters into what one eminent psychoanalyst has called a "conspiracy of silence" about these and other critical childhood experiences, he only heightens a child's confusions and worries. Adult evasion and concealment shake a child's trust and intensify his fears. While he knows that something is wrong, he knows also that his parents feel it is wrong to ask about it. And when he is not helped to bring his fears, fantasies, confusions out into the open so that they can be discussed and corrected, then ultimately they are repressed. But that does not mean that the feelings have disappeared. They are still part of him.

When Jonathan Fuller was five years old, his father suffered a mild heart attack and was ordered to the hospital for a few weeks. Naturally, Mrs. Fuller was concerned about her husband and was greatly relieved when the doctor was able to tell her that he would recover. Still, all she could bring herself to say to Jonathan was: "Daddy will be fine, dear, and home before we know it."

Certainly Mrs. Fuller could not be expected to give young Jonathan a detailed medical report, but by saying only the bare minimum, and making it clear that this was a subject she would rather not discuss,—she actually, without meaning to, made the whole situation more painful for him, rather than less so. To the little sum of knowledge Jonathan did possess, he added the powerful ingredients of his own imagination. By not allowing his feelings to come out and be talked about, his mother provided no way to ease his inner suffering.

Jonathan was not sure that perhaps his father had gone away because he was angry with him for demanding so much of his mother's attention. He even believed that perhaps he was to blame for the heart attack. Jonathan carried all these burdens himself and because his feelings were so painful to him, he finally buried them. But they are still part of him and they may well come out later on in one disturbing form or another.

The Sunday afternoon an automobile hit eight-year-old Ellen Morse, terror struck the entire Morse household as well. Ellen's mother and father and Julie, her ten-year-old sister, all drove to the hospital together. It was an anxious time for them until they learned that Ellen had come out of the accident with nothing more serious than a fractured leg and wrist. It could have been much worse. The next day at school Julie acted disturbed and unhappy. She could not answer any of the geography questions, she got a low mark on her arithmetic test, she was moody at recess time. All this was perfectly understandable—after all, she was upset by Ellen's accident and worried about her. But when more than a week went by and Julie continued to look and act not at all like herself, her parents knew that she was deeply troubled. They had never known Julie to rush right up to her room after school, as she often did these days, and to stay there alone for an hour or two. And her schoolwork was becoming erratic—excellent one day, poor the next.

Encouraged by her parents to talk about what was

bothering her, Julie finally blurted out: "Ellen's accident was all my fault. If I'd taken her to the movies with me that Sunday, it wouldn't have happened."

Magical thinking

Even a ten-year-old like Julie sometimes has residues of early magical thinking, the belief that wishes can actually cause things to happen. And in Julie's case traces of her jealousy of her younger sister, which had often in the past made her wish Ellen would go away, were still around to plague her and cause her this present guilt and unhappiness In addition, she resented the extra attention Ellen was receiving, but until now had been afraid to say so.

As Julie talked about her inner feelings, the weight of the world seemed to fall from her. Naturally, not everything was cleared up by this one discussion, but day by day as Julie's parents patiently encouraged her to talk about those fears and worries that had arisen after Ellen's accident, they helped her to set things straight and to lessen her anxieties. Had they not encouraged her to express her "dark thoughts," Julie might well have taken their silence for secret agreement with her that she really was the cause of her sister's accident.

Is there a connection between these examples and the development of ethical behavior? Indeed there is. To do right a child must feel right and he cannot feel right when he is harboring a horde of secret fears and worries. Not all children react the same way to family crises and difficulties, but when parents listen carefully to what their children say, and, even more important, what they do not say, they can very often find out what is on their minds and what may be troubling them. Then they can make many opportunities to break through the barrier of silence and let worries and conflicts come out into the open where they can be dealt with as they arise.

Difficult explanations

Separation and divorce are among the hardest things to talk to children about. Many conscientious parents, having reached a carefully thought out decision that separating is the best course for them, still put off telling the children. Often they say it is to spare their youngsters pain for as long as possible, though probably their own understandable guilt and fear are what keep them silent. But evasion can continue for only so long and it is usually much worse for a child than the shock of hearing the truth, hard as that is. No one would deny that children do best in a home with a mother and father who love and enjoy each other and them. But no parent needs to feel that he has done his child irreparable harm if his marriage must be dissolved. No real evidence exists to prove that children cannot turn out well when divorced parents disregard their own personal antagonisms and continue to act together in the best interests of the children. And very real evidence does exist that children from unbroken, but unhappy, homes often fare very badly indeed.

When Maud and Allen Heller decided to tell their two sons, Jack, nine and Harry, seven, that they were getting a divorce, it was not easy for them, but they were surprised at their relief when it was finally out in the open. They told the children just as much as they could. Maud said something like this to the boys: "Dad and I both love you very much, but the two of us are so unhappy together that we know it will be better for us to stop being married. That doesn't mean that we stop being your mother and father or stop taking care of you." Allen felt it was important to tell his sons exactly what the plans were: that Jack and Harry would still live in the same house with their mother; still go to the same school; that, of course, they could call him at the office as usual; that he would visit them every Sunday; that they would spend some of their summer vacation with him.

The Hellers realized full well that just making this careful explanation at the outset was not going to prevent all difficulties for the boys or keep them from being unhappy. They did feel, however, that making the plans extremely clear to the youngsters would lessen their initial confusion.

But the story had to be told over and over again. Some days the boys seemed to realize that their parents would never live together again. Other days they acted as though it were not true. Answering their questions was difficult, convincing them of the finality of the decision was harder still. Each parent was scrupulous to avoid undermining the other whenever they talked with the boys about the divorce. Many complex and difficult adjustments had to be made as Jack and Harry finally came to accept the fact that their father was no longer going to be a part of the household. They were often angry and resentful—sometimes at him, sometimes at their mother. The truth could not be made painless for the boys, but the Hellers managed to keep the pain from being destructive. Both parents, even though they were living apart, continued to do all they could to make the boys feel loved and secure and protected. Far from an ideal situation, it nevertheless worked out reasonably well for Jack and Harry because all of their needs were taken into account and their questions and fears were not shrouded in silence.

Not all (in fact, not many) divorced parents can handle the situation for their children as well as the Hellers did, or talk about it as openly. Separation or divorce is a disturbing experience for any child, and it can have far-reaching effects on his emotional and ethical development. Whether or not it will do serious harm to a child depends very largely on how the whole matter is handled. A child needs to feel that both his parents are good people and that they love him, even though they themselves may not have been able to get along together. Very often skilled help is necessary to spare children from serious emotional turmoil and to undo any damage that may already have been done. It is wise for parents who face these problems to seek such help from a psychiatrist, or a family service or counseling agency.

When death occurs

Fewer and fewer young children these days are likely to have any direct contact with death. Still they hear about it from friends or neighbors, see it on TV, and are often puzzled and concerned even when it has not touched their lives directly. Many parents find it difficult to talk about death but by keeping silent about it, they only increase a child's fears and confusions. Ordinarily, very young children neither need nor want detailed explanations. Simple, matter-of-fact information in answer to their questions serves them best. But if death does occur in their own family, silence or evasion does not keep them from realizing that something very important has happened and from being affected by it. They become aware that death causes grief and they are often shaken, especially if no explanations are forthcoming, at seeing their parents overcome by sorrow.

When six-year-old Evie Cole's grandmother died, her mother could not bring herself to talk about it or to answer Evie's questions. She thought it best to say simply that Grandma was old and tired and was taking a long, long rest. But Evie sensed that there was something peculiar about this "rest" that her mother wanted to keep secret from her. After a week of having trouble getting Evie to take a rest or to stay quietly in bed at night as she used to do, Mrs. Cole made the connection: Evie was fighting resting and sleeping because then she, too, might take a long, long rest like Grandma's.

Then Mrs. Cole explained it again to Evie. She told her that she now realized that Evie could understand a little more about Grandma's death, and she cleared up the matter of a "long, long rest." By making it all less mysterious and hence less frightening to Evie, she relieved her of her disturbing fantasy. Even more important, she got across to her that it was all right to ask these questions, and any others that might be troubling her. Evie absorbed as much of what her mother told her as she was ready for. She is likely to feel freer to bring other worries to her mother now that she knows it is all right to talk about them. Knowing that her mother will listen and help her understand gives her courage.

The question that eight-year-old Jean Dillman put to her mother was heartbreaking. "What is going to happen to poor Grandpa in that box," Jean wanted to know. "Will the worms eat him up?"

The very thought of her beloved father's body eventually disintegrating was too painful for Mrs. Dillman to think about, let alone talk about freely with Jean. Wisely, she decided to let Jean's father answer the child's questions.

By explaining in simple terms what happens to a body after death, Mr. Dillman uncovered and corrected some of Jean's confusions. It helped her to know that Grandpa's body could not feel anything now, that he himself had known for a long time that everyone finally dies, and that this is what happens to bodies that are no longer alive. It comforted Jean to have her father tell her that she and the baby and her parents were probably going to be around for a long, long time. And because her father missed Grandpa and said so, but did not seem overly troubled by the fact of death, Jean was helped to understand and to feel less threatened herself. When her mother no longer had to conceal her grief from Jean, it somehow gave the child permission to share in it a little, and to learn that grief, just as much as happiness, was a feeling one could show. All this helped Jean to overcome the shock of Grandpa's death.

Parents who derive comfort from a belief in the hereafter will naturally share this faith with their children.

Those who are less certain can help their youngsters by emphasizing the continuing influence of the person who has died in the lives of all who loved him. The important thing is to give children opportunities to ask questions and to express their thoughts and feelings. Without words, fears cannot be talked about and you may be unwittingly withholding needed comfort and courage from your youngsters by your silence, however well intentioned.

Explaining mental illness

Mrs. Goldman was understandably distressed when it became necessary to send her young brother to a mental hospital. Her twelve-year-old son Charley was especially fond of his Uncle Ted, and she could not bring herself to tell him why her brother was hospitalized.

Ted's illness was not unknown in the neighborhood. It took only a few days before a schoolmate taunted Charley about his uncle who "had to be sent away because he was nuts." But it took Charley nearly a week to tell his mother what he had learned, and it had been anguish for him the whole time. He was beset with fears that he had "bad blood" and would "go crazy" just like Uncle Ted.

Mrs. Goldman realized how wrong she had been in keeping silent about Ted. She decided to sit down with Charley and talk it out calmly. She told him that expressions like "crazy" and "bad blood" were used by frightened and ignorant people who did not understand what they were talking about.

"I was frightened myself at first," she said. "That's probably why I kept the truth from you. You don't need to worry about getting Ted's illness. It's not inherited. His doctors know what's wrong and they are helping him to get well."

It took more talking about the whole problem to give Charley a clearer idea of the situation, to realize that it was nothing to be ashamed of, and to calm his fears. Parental silence in Charley's case was indeed something less than golden, as it is with most children. When the lines of communication between children and parents are kept open, almost all questions can be satisfactorily handled. Of course, parents should not go overboard and tell a child more than he can take, but the confusions that arise out of silence can be far more painful than the truth. Children need to feel that neither their questions nor the feelings accompanying them are so unacceptable that they cannot be talked about. Younger children, especially, need to feel that their parents are strong enough to deal with whatever is troubling them.

Parents remain silent about many questions that do not involve family crises, for example, children's curiosity about their bodies and about sex. In Chapter II, *Glad to be a Boy . . . Proud to be a Girl* we discussed the importance of satisfying this curiosity, and letting youngsters know there is nothing shameful about their interest or their feelings. But to expect a child to have the courage to bring up subjects which his parents never raise is to expect him to be stronger than they are. Parents have to have the imagination to know when their children are interested and curious but also afraid to ask questions. By helping them put into words their doubts and uncertainties, they not only make their youngsters feel better, they are also helping them along the road to ethical behavior.

Financial crises

When Mr. Ellis lost his job, he and his wife decided not to tell the children. They could manage on his unemployment compensation and their savings for a while until he got a new job, and they wanted to protect nine-year-old Forest and eleven-year-old Frannie from worry. Mrs. Ellis was careful not to mention a word of her anxiety to the children, but it could not help showing through in her face and in her manner. Both Forest and Frannie knew that something was wrong, but they did not ask about it because their parents had not brought it up first.

But Mr. Ellis was out of work for a longer period of time than he had thought he would be. He and his wife realized that they could not continue to be silent about the situation.

"Kids," Mr. Ellis said, "I'm going to need your help. We're all going to have to be more careful with money until I get a new job." He encouraged them to ask questions which helped them get rid of their anxieties and he gave them honest and thoughtful answers. Both children needed to feel that their parents could deal with this emergency and that they would all come through all right.

Instead of being miserable, the youngsters actually were relieved at knowing the truth and were heartened by hearing that they could be helpful. They volunteered to cut out movies and sodas and, of course, not to ask for anything new for the duration. When Mr. Ellis got a new job several weeks later, the celebration dinner they all had was one of the gayest parties of their lives. Even though Forest and Frannie have now grown to adulthood, they still talk about it as one of the most happy and unifying events of their childhood.

Rows between parents

Mothers and fathers may not realize how even an occasional parental spat can be misinterpreted by a young child when it occurs in his presence. Even the most happily married couples (this is no news flash!) do give vent to anger or irritation when their children are around. Four-year-old Marie Johnson was coloring her Mother Goose book in a corner of the living room, not really listening to her mother and father talking as they went over their plans for the new house. But as their voices got louder and louder, Marie sat up from her coloring book, tense and rigid. The next minute her father strode to the front door and slammed it hard behind him. Marie looked inquiringly at her mother whose face was blazing. Then her eyes filled up with tears.

Mrs. Johnson picked up Marie and talked to her sooth-ingly. "Yes, dear," she replied to her sobbed out question, "Daddy and I did get mad at each other. But he'll be back in a few minutes, and it will all be over. Then the three of us can have a cocoa party."

By her simple explanation of the outburst, Mrs. Johnson calmed Marie's fright. She was not ashamed to tell her that mothers and fathers, like everybody else, do get angry with each other once in a while. And because Marie was aware of the overall happiness and contentment in the Johnson household, this unaccustomed blowup did not affect her for long. Her mother's few words, instead of strained silence, were just what Marie needed to hear.

(Of course, if parents constantly argue and battle, a child's chances of developing healthy feelings of right and wrong, or of acquiring any other desirable attitudes, are seriously threatened. Continued quarreling terrifies chil-dren. Not only do they want to escape from such an at-mosphere, but constant disparagement of one parent by the other confuses them and puts nearly unbearable strains on their love and loyalty.)

Uncertainty is worse than unpleasantness

More and more parents are coming to realize that chil-dren feel much more threatened by the unknown, by their fears and confusions than they are by uncertainties, no matter how unpleasant. Children gain strength when their parents share with them, to some extent at least, the bad as well as the good. Through knowing that they can be talked to and trusted, youngsters develop a sense of their own worth and a boost along the road to ethical behavior. Even more important, when parents break down the barriers of silence that surround many things—death, divorce, illness, sex—they give their children permission to talk about their fears and confusions.

What is talked about can be corrected, but when there

are no words and no sharing, clarification becomes impossible. Parents do not shy away from talking about difficult subjects and uncovering misapprehensions because they deliberately want to confuse their children. As has always been the case, most mothers and fathers love their youngsters and want to do their best for them. But it is often more comfortable for parents to go on pretending that something is not so by remaining silent about it. Once they put it into words, this is no longer possible. It takes courage to bring some things out into the open, but generally what parents do not talk about first, most children will not be able to bring up themselves.

Earlier in this chapter we saw how a child can mistakenly feel that some unhappy event may well be the result of his own wishes or behavior. When this is so, and no attempts have been made to talk openly about the situation, a youngster may develop a sense of guilt and unhappiness that can plague him all his life. It is usually best to explain unpleasant happenings briefly and promptly, answering children's questions honestly and in language they can understand. This often difficult, but necessary, course helps a child to know right from wrong and to grow to ethical maturity. Thoughtful parents will want to break down this potentially harmful "conspiracy of silence."

Chapter eleven

ONCE MORE WITH FEELING

When the bonds between parents and their children are strong and loving and provide the incentives for ethical behavior, there is good reason to believe that youngsters will come to know right from wrong and will generally be able to act on their knowledge. But the road to mature ethical conduct is long and rocky. By way of summary, let us take a hypothetical Johnny and follow his progress along this road.

Johnny comes into the world with no sense of right and wrong, good and evil, as his parents understand these concepts. For Johnny, good is what gives him pleasure, and bad is what gives him pain. Life is good when his mother feeds him, picks him up, cuddles him. Life is bad when he is hungry, wet, uncomfortable. As his mother cares for him and meets his needs promptly and lovingly, young Johnny, aware now that she is a separate being from himself, develops confidence in her. His needs, his comfort, are important—*he* is important and cared for.

Before the end of his first year Johnny starts to acquire a significant ingredient in ethical behavior. Ever so slightly he can begin to defer gratification—to wait a bit now, though not for long, to be fed or changed or played with. He anticipates that his needs will be met because they have been met. All during this first year as Johnny's mother gives him his share of loving attention and companionship, he develops a basic sense of trust in her, and in his environment. Aware of it or not, she is already nurturing the seeds of a potentially ethical human being.

Between two and three, Johnny is the Big Explorer, the Constant Inquirer. His imagination is strong and outstrips his ability to deal with it. He is not certain where the real ends and the unreal begins. Knowing this, his mother guides him gently and firmly. Trouble looms up on all sides as his healthy curiosity spurs him to learn by touching and grabbing and tasting practically everything within reach. Johnny's mother knows that his curiosity is natural and does not turn it into a battle of wills. She does not let the situation develop into such a struggle. She could always win the contest, but that would neither encourage Johnny to find out about the world around him nor prepare him for self-control.

Knowing that he has a long way to go before he understands the "rules" or can follow them, his mother tries to make this period in his growth easier on him and on her. She holds back on too many No's, clears his path of dangerous, untouchable items, and gives him as much space as possible for free activity.

His parents enjoy Johnny and show their pride in his accomplishments. They answer his questions and encourage his interests. By not blocking his every move with restrictions and disapproval, they prepare Johnny to move ahead with confidence. But he is not yet equipped to understand right or wrong except in terms of what gives him pleasure or pain.

Life becomes harder for Johnny with the arrival of a baby sister. With skill and patience his parents let him know that he is not being displaced in their affections. Understanding that he is jealous of the baby, they help him handle his feelings without shaming him or making him feel guilty. They let him know unmistakably that hitting the baby is wrong and forbidden, even though he might very well feel like it at times. Through words and actions they convince Johnny that he is still very important to them, that they love him as much as ever.

Being able to communicate more and to express himself have given Johnny some measure of control. Encouraged by his parents to talk about the things that bother him, he feels less ashamed of his "bad" feelings and more certain of his worth. Right now his parents' love and approval are his strongest incentives to good behavior. He does not always understand why some of his actions cause their disapproval, but he is learning to avoid doing what displeases them.

By the time Johnny is five he is on his way to having a real sense of right and wrong of his own. He has learned that his parents love him, even though they restrain him when he misbehaves. They know that it is not love to permit him to do anything and everything he pleases. They understand that love without demands—or demands without love—would impede, not foster, his ethical development.

Rugged times

Before Johnny goes off to school and to new influences on his ethical growth, we might stop and ask: Was all of this as easy as it may sound? Were Johnny's parents paragons? Did each stage run smoothly into the next? Of course not. There were many trouble spots along the way. Many times Johnny's mother and father were irritated, angry, unsure of themselves. And problems that seemed solved one month cropped up again the next and had to be dealt with over and over again. Hard times were inevitable as Johnny grew and developed.

Probably the hardest time for Johnny and his parents during this preschool period came when they brought the new baby back from the hospital. Johnny was a cheerful two-and-a-half then and things had been going along exceedingly well. Now all at once everything seemed to go wrong. Johnny began to whine a lot. He often refused to feed himself—which he had been doing for some time now with great pride. His mother, understanding Johnny's need to act like a baby again, let him and was patient—even when she was dog-tired. She tried in every way she knew to convince him that she and his father loved him just as much as they did his new sister. Things began to look up for awhile, and they thought Johnny understood. Then he developed a new trick. He began coming out of bed at night, asking for a drink of water or demanding one more story. After a long and tiring day, this was too much. The first night, after it happened three times, Johnny's mother scolded him severely and finally sent him back to bed in tears. Nothing daunted, he reappeared for the fourth time, acting as though he had spent the whole day on the Sahara.

His accusing look implied that only the most cruel tyrant in the world would deny him a drink.

Even though Johnny's parents knew that he needed the reassurance of their love (and their company), they were harsh with him for two or three nights in a row as he continued this new performance. But they felt guilty about their severity. Anyway it did no good—Johnny still kept right on coming out. They decided to change their tactics. His mother began by taking him back to bed promptly and without argument or fuss each time he came out. She no longer scolded him as she let him know what was expected of him. In addition, she managed to work out a rearrangement of the baby's schedule which gave her more time for Johnny's good-night story and all his bedtime routines.

It seemed ages before Johnny stopped popping out of bed, but the combination of sympathy and firmness, along with frequent reassurance that Johnny's feelings about his sister were all right and understandable, finally turned the trick. Still and all, it was a rugged time and Johnny's mother still has a few qualms about her handling of the problem. She has learned that practically nothing gets settled once and for all.

There were lots of other ups and downs before Johnny reached school age, times when it seemed hard to point him in the direction of right and away from wrong without squelching his spirit or shaming him. Small crises occurred with exasperating regularity—toilet lapses, temper tantrums, feeding difficulties. Sometimes Johnny's mother handled them in ways that she was proud of. Other times she was not so sure. Mistakes or not, her over-all handling was firm and friendly, and that was what counted.

At six, Johnny was a happy and steady youngster with an emerging sense of right and wrong and increasing possibilities for self-control. It was clear that he liked being a boy. His love for his father was seen in the way he

167

copied his remarks and imitated his behavior. Johnny's standards of good and bad were still very largely determined by what his family said and did, but soon his friends and teachers would be important influences on his ethical growth.

Johnny's first few years in school were for the most part on the plus side. He did reasonably well, and his parents and teachers were proud of him. He gained satisfaction from his accomplishments, and his self-confidence grew. He made several close friends whose good opinion he wanted very much to keep. He got into a small bout with his sense of right and wrong when he joined with two of his pals in swiping some apples from the corner grocery stand because he did not want to be considered a sissy. He was relieved that he did not have to do it again and that his parents never found out about it. On more than one occasion he was torn by conflicting loyalties.

As Johnny moved further along into the preteens his mother and father sometimes wondered if he had forgotten everything they had taught him. A little reflection convinced them that while Johnny now had periods of being insolent and sloppy and had picked up large amounts of tough talk, he actually had learned well what they considered acceptable behavior. If he had not, he would not be bothering to protest against it. More important than the occasional scrapes Johnny got into were the evidences of his strong feelings of kindness and sympathy—basic building blocks for a sound ethical character.

Currently Johnny is demonstrating his shift to his own age group for his models of behavior. His self-assertion is a healthy sign of his growing independence and his emerging critical judgment. While his parents give him a reasonable amount of leeway, they never let him get away with murder. They know that even when he protests, he still needs their love and approval. Not all the time, but a good deal

168

of it, his mother and father manage a combination of firmness, love, and understanding.

While he teases his sister unmercifully at times, his affection for her is clearly triumphing over his old resentment. As Johnny works at putting together his experiences and trying to incorporate a set of values into his life, his ethical sense grows. Sorting out his feelings and thoughts, his observations and conflicts, is no easy job. His ethical growth has been uneven and sporadic, but it is building. Although Johnny's sense of right and wrong is now a stable part of his personality, he will not be ready to take over full control by himself until the end of adolescence.

As he moves into high school, Johnny has the usual assortment of teen-age conflicts—no more, no less. He is trying hard right now to find out who he is and what he stands for. He is beginning to think more critically than before about many ethical problems. Even though he confides less in his parents these days, he usually has a good feeling about them as they back him up in his desire for eventual independence.

Parent-child relationships, the key to ethical behavior

This telescoped glimpse of Johnny's continuing ethical progress reveals its most important element: the quality of the relationship between Johnny and his family. Even more than the good examples his parents set for him, vital though these were, or the ethical principles they taught him (and these, too, were necessary), was the underlying good feeling that was always there despite the inevitable ups and downs. When his parents got angry, when they made mistakes, when they were unsure of which course was best, they always got across to him that they valued him for himself—for the single, unduplicated individual that was

Johnny. Without this sure knowledge and the deep, warm ties that existed within his family, Johnny's progress toward ethical maturity would have been in serious jeopardy. Overloading him with platitudes about honesty or kindness would not have made Johnny honest and kind. He develops these qualities through the feelings he acquires as his parents treat him honestly and kindly, and he learns in great part through his feelings.

The quality of parent-child relationships is what counts most. It explains why even a criminal who is good to his children may bring up youngsters who know right from wrong and can act on it, and why a clergyman, who is harsh and severe with his youngsters, may bring them up to be delinquents or criminals.

The value of flexibility

Over the years, Johnny—like all normal youngsters—showed the capacity to adapt and to change. This is important for all parents to remember. No single unfortunate experience need preclude a child's developing a sense of right and wrong. No single event is so powerful that it forces a child into a rigid pattern of feeling and acting. New patterns can be established, old ones corrected.

Parents, too, learn as they go along. Realizing that what works for someone else's child may not work for theirs, they come to find out what is best for their own youngsters and their own particular situation. If they are flexible and change their tactics when it seems advisable, they gain confidence from their experiences in facing and meeting problems. When problems seem insurmountable, they are less reluctant than parents used to be to turn for professional help and guidance. They realize that seeking advice is not a sign that they have failed, but that on the contrary, knowing when help is needed is a sign of understanding and intelligence.

Perhaps it is not too much to hope that as more and more children grow to ethical maturity, their sense of right and wrong will be felt in the world at large. Loving, co-operative, and trusting, they will want to help build a loving, co-operative, and trusting world. At what other time in history has the world been in such urgent need of these qualities of love and sympathy, justice and fairness, courage and loyalty that constitute ethical conduct?

Appendix I

YOUR CHILD'S HEALTH

Naturally parents are concerned about the physical health of their children as well as their emotional and ethical development. For this reason it seems advisable to include as Appendix I to this book some basic health information as well as a guide to the common communicable diseases of childhood.

Your own feelings about health—as about everything else—affect your children. Some mothers are overanxious and fussy, others act coldly "scientific." Those who can steer a middle course help their children develop a healthy attitude toward their own health and encourage them to assume reasonable responsibility for it when they are ready.

For the brand-new American citizen who is born as you are reading this, the gift of life may well span seventy years or longer. He and his contemporaries are safe from many serious diseases which once snuffed out thousands of young lives every single year. Right from early infancy, the protective shield of inoculation guards children against many infections and helps keep our communities free from epidemics.

No way is yet known to prevent for certain what are called the "common childhood diseases": measles, German measles, mumps, and chickenpox. Since these infections are relatively mild for most children, it is better for Johnny or Susie to catch them while they are young, thus developing an active immunity against them that usually lasts for a lifetime. Some doctors advise deliberately exposing young girls to German measles because this disease, if caught by a woman during the first three months of pregnancy, may harm her unborn baby.

Babies up to two months of age seem to have a certain natural immunity to most diseases except whooping cough. So some time around the second month of your baby's life is the ideal time for inoculations against diphtheria, tetanus, whooping cough, smallpox, and polio. Shots for diphtheria, whooping cough, and tetanus are now conveniently combined in a mixture of triple vaccine that simultaneously immunizes against all three diseases. Some physicians like to use a quadruple vaccine which includes the polio inoculation. It is expected that oral vaccine for polio will soon be licensed and in good supply.

If your child is past babyhood and has not yet had his shots, you will want to start now. Since no single inoculation can give permanent immunity to any disease, first shots must be reinforced with boosters given at definite intervals later on. So for easy future reference it is a good idea to keep a record of the dates of your child's injections. (See p. 181.)

When you take your baby to the doctor for his shots, expect the needle prick to hurt or startle him, at least momentarily. Your reassuring hug and maybe a favorite toy, brought along for the occasion, will help comfort him. Some toddlers, depending on temperament, may kick up quite a fuss about getting shots. Here, too, your calm and sympathetic attitude is a "salve" that helps heal the hurt.

After receiving his shots, a child may have a slight but temporary reaction—a sore arm or inflammation where the injection was given, and a little fever. This simply means that the child's system is working to build up necessary immunity. It is usually nothing to worry about. To help him feel more comfortable, your doctor may suggest giving him a small amount of crushed aspirin.

You will find the charts on pp. 182-185 a useful guide to help you recognize the common childhood diseases.

Once a child is past infancy, parents are sometimes tempted to neglect the periodic health examination. This is poor economy. Competent medical supervision is worth taking time and trouble to obtain and may save money and worry in the end. When the doctor sees a child regularly he can be on the lookout for even more than signs of physical difficulties, important though they are. He also has an opportunity to learn what the child is like socially, emotionally, and intellectually. Also you will want to introduce your child to the family dentist when he is around three, so that the dentist can win his confidence and co-operation and can allay any fears he may have at a time when little, if any, dental work need be done.

Mothers often worry needlessly about their young children's eating habits. Eating problems are generally not as serious as parents fear, and they can almost always be helped. Because you know how important food is, it is natural for you to be concerned about what your child eats and how much he eats.

Trouble often arises when a child doesn't want to drink his milk or when he refuses to finish what is on his plate. This is the time to remember not to make an issue of his refusal. Remember that you, too, don't always want the exact amount of food placed before you. Imagine what an ordeal your own mealtime would become if someone were always standing over you coaxing or scolding you to finish your cereal or eat all your vegetables.

It's occasionally a good idea to offer a child a smaller portion of a food that he has previously refused or to serve it early in the meal while he is still hungry. Try to include in each meal at least one food that he especially likes.

If there are foods that he especially dislikes, substitute others. If he dislikes cereals, give him wholewheat toast for a while. If he refuses to drink milk at some time, don't make a fuss but use it in soups and custards. If he obviously dislikes milk, consult your doctor. Milk may disagree with your youngster; it does with some children. If he hates certain vegetables, give him others or fruits with the same properties. One good way to get a child finally to accept all kinds of foods is not to try to make him eat everything but to allow him some freedom of choice.

Sometimes difficulties occur when children are expected to eat too much. The amount of food a child needs depends in part on how fast he is growing. Children grow and develop at different rates at different ages. The child who is in a period when he is growing at a slower rate may need and want less food than the faster growing child. Your doctor can tell you how much food is right for your child. If your youngster doesn't eat as much as your neighbor's child does, it's not necessarily something to worry about. Just remember that no two children are alike and that the child whose appetite is smaller may be getting enough to eat for his own particular needs.

Various things may interfere with your child's normal

desire for food. Notice when these times are and try to think what the cause may be. Was he excited? Was he overtired? If he was, then he might well want to eat less than usual. If changes have occurred in the household, such as moving or someone going away or the arrival of a new baby, his anxiety might be reflected in his eating. Almost any emotional disturbance could make him difficult about his food, and to force him to eat if he is upset would only make further trouble. Occasionally, there may be some physical reason why a child does not eat well, but this is not generally the case. In any event, you will want to check with your doctor to make sure your child has no particular physical problems.

Sometimes children go in for food fads and develop peculiar notions about eating. A child may, for a short period of time, want only liquids or uncooked food or no vegetables. Just as with other eating problems, food fads are likely to disappear more quickly if you do not make them seem like something tremendously important. Don't be discouraged if improvement is slow. There are bound to be setbacks, but if they are handled wisely, improvement will gradually take place. If you can make mealtime a pleasant time—a time without strain or hurry—and if you offer good food in a casual, friendly way, without urging, you will have gone a long way toward helping your child develop good eating habits.

During the first year or so at school your youngster is likely to get a few colds and other respiratory ills, and to catch the common communicable diseases. At this age, children usually recover promptly and gradually build up considerable resistance.

Teeth continue to need attention. Some permanent teeth are erupting, and cavities can develop surprisingly fast during any period of rapid bone growth. Your child's teeth should be cleaned by a dentist at least twice a year, and

176

they should be examined for crookedness or malocclusion (upper and lower teeth which do not come together properly) as well as cavities.

Some parents stop supplementing a child's regular diet with concentrated vitamins and minerals around this time. It is a good idea to let your physician be the judge of whether your youngster gets enough of what he needs for proper growth and development from his usual meals. By the time they enter school most youngsters are eating more heartily and with greater willingness to experiment, so it is a good time to reintroduce foods that they may have felt a dislike or prejudice toward earlier.

Around this age children generally need about eleven to twelve hours of sleep. Some children also need a brief daytime nap or rest period before fatigue sets in too deeply. Since many of them now resist taking a real nap, it is a good idea to intersperse occasional periods of quiet play or reading or talking, especially in the late afternoon.

Sensible, but not overcautious, stress on health precautions at home will supplement that given primary-graders in school. Covering nose and mouth for sneezes or coughs should be pointed out as a thoughtful protection for others. Disposable tissues should be provided, and disposal right after use emphasized. Since so many childhood diseases start out with symptoms that look like "just a little cold," it is safer to ask the doctor than to trust to guesswork if you are in doubt.

Choosing the proper clothing for each day's weather can become a morning source of argument. Children of this age notice what others wear, and they want to wear the same things. Sometimes it helps to have mothers discuss among themselves what appropriate protective clothing their children need. Once they agree, some of the problems disappear. No child wants to be the *only* one wearing boots and a snowsuit on a reasonably mild day. But on the other hand, he does not want to be the only one *not* wearing a sou'wester on a torrential one. Here the desire to conform can become a real health asset, once parents agree on the same kind of plan.

When your youngster gets to be nine or ten, he will probably have had his quota of mumps, measles, and chicken pox. But it is still as important as ever to schedule regular health check-ups with your child's physician to detect or prevent any difficulties before they develop. And you'll remember regular dental appointments, too.

Except for a few who mature early, the preteens grow steadily, but slowly. By the time they are eleven, the girls are at least a full year ahead of the boys. They begin their preteen spurt in height and weight earlier, but the boys will overtake them a little later on. This is not much comfort at the moment to your daughter if she is taller than any of the boys in her class, but you can promise her that in a couple of years' time the boys will not only catch up, but most of them will get ahead of her. But two years can seem like two centuries to her while she is waiting.

By the time your youngster is in his teens he is ready to take on more and more responsibility for his own health. Naturally you are still concerned, but often in a teenager's mind parental emphasis on health habits is connected with "babying." If you overstress health precautions, he may have to defy you to "prove" how tough and invulnerable he is. The same basic principles of diet, rest, exercise, and cleanliness that apply to younger and older people apply to adolescents as well. Many teen-agers sometimes worry over being too fat or too thin, too short or too tall, and they frequently need help in understanding that they are not abnormal just because their timetable of growth is different from that of their friends. Too, they often need to be reassured that bigness or littleness has nothing to do with "dumbness" or "smartness."

Many adolescents worry about their complexions and are miserable if their faces are broken out with the blackheads and pimples of acne. You can do a great deal to help your teen-ager make the most of his looks during this time. Your family doctor will be of real help here. He can often prescribe medication and specific skin care to clear up a blotched complexion, and he can suggest a diet that will also help. Regular medical examinations and consultations can be especially valuable at adolescence. They give the doctor a chance to see that the youngster is growing normally, to detect any signs of difficulty—physical or emotional—and to see that he gets needed treatment, if any is indicated. When there is nothing seriously wrong, just being told by his doctor that he is all right is often the only medicine a teen-ager needs.

One of the great advances of modern medicine is its recognition of the importance of emotions in influencing bodily health. This view recognizes that mind and body work together as one (not as separate units), with the body reacting upon the mind, and the mind upon the body. Illness develops when the symptoms become involuntary.

Parents can practice an important bit of preventive medicine by applying this knowledge with their children. Your attitudes, as we have shown throughout this book, are all-important. We have seen how excessive leniency, excessive anxiety, excessive harshness can all do damage in different ways. As you know, childhood is not always the happy, carefree time of life some adults, looking back, like to imagine it was. Most grownups have forgotten many of their childhood tragedies because they were too painful to remember. But many adults suffer ill health and a host of other difficulties whose roots can be traced back to those early childhood days.

When parents give their children love, offer them sympathetic understanding as well as firm guidance, and permit them to show their feelings and to talk about them, they help protect their youngsters from some of the disturbances common among adults today. Parents must continue to give their children physical immunization, but they can also give them a large measure of "emotional immunization" as well.

Record of injections

Names of Children:			
Birth Date:			
Polio 1			
2			
3			
4			
Boosters			
Diphtheria ⎫ 1			
Tetanus ⎬ 2			
Whooping ⎭ 3 Cough			
Boosters			
Smallpox 1			
2			
3			
Revaccinations			

Communicable diseases of childhood*

DISEASE	CHICKEN POX	DIPHTHERIA
Cause	A virus: present in secretions from nose, throat, mouth of infected people.	Diphtheria bacillus: present in secretions from nose, throat, and skin of infected people and carriers.
How spread	Contact with infected people or articles used by them. Very contagious.	Contact with infected people and carriers or articles used by them.
Incubation period (from date of exposure to first signs)	14 to 16 days. Sometimes 3 weeks.	2 to 5 days. Sometimes longer.
Period of communicability (time when disease is contagious)	From about 1 day before to 6 days after first appearance of skin blisters.	From about 2 to 4 weeks after onset of disease.
Most susceptible ages	Common under 15 years.	Common under 10 years.
Seasons of prevalence	Winter.	Fall and winter.
Prevention	None.	Inoculation with diphtheria toxoid (in triple or quadruple vaccine for babies).
Control	Isolation during period of communicability but not essential to isolate until all skin crusts are gone. Cut child's fingernails short and keep clean. Immunity usual after one attack.	Isolation until 3 cultures from nose and throat taken at 24-hour intervals are free of bacilli. Antibiotics and antitoxin used in treatment and for protection after exposure. One attack does not necessarily give immunity.

* Based on 1960 Report of Committee on Control of Infectious Diseases. American A

GERMAN MEASLES	INFANTILE PARALYSIS	MEASLES
A virus: present in secretions from nose and mouth of infected people.	Three strains of polio virus have been identified: present in discharges from nose, throat, bowels of infected people.	A virus: present in secretions from nose and throat of infected people.
Contact with infected people or articles used by them. Very contagious.	Contact with infected people.	Contact with infected people or articles used by them. Very contagious.
14 to 25 (usually 18) days.	About 7 to 21 days.	7 to 14 (usually 12 to 13) days.
From about 4 days after onset of symptoms.	Apparently greatest in late incubation and first few days of acute illness.	From 2 to 7 days after onset of first symptoms.
Young children.	Most common in children 1 to 16 years; prevalent in young adults.	Common at any age during childhood.
Spring and winter.	June through September.	Mainly spring. Also fall and winter.
None.	Polio vaccine.	None. Protective shots sometimes given within 3 days after exposure to avert or lighten attack.
Isolation, when necessary, from first symptoms until 2 days after appearance of rash. No attempt should be made to protect young girls from this disease. No control. Immunity usual after one attack.	Isolation (differs by state law) for about one week from onset, for duration of fever. Immunity to infecting strain of virus usual after one attack.	Isolation during period of communicability. Antibiotics sometimes used in treatment. Immunity usual after one attack.

of Pediatrics, and Metropolitan Life Insurance Company's *ABC's of Childhood Disease.*

Communicable diseases of childhood (Continued)

DISEASE	MUMPS	"STREP" INFECTIONS
Cause	A virus: present in saliva of infected people.	Streptococci of several strains cause scarlet fever, and "strep" sore throats: present in secretions from mouth, nose, ears, of infected people and carriers.
How spread	Contact with infected people or articles used by them.	Contact with infected people and carriers. Also from dust, lint, contaminated food and milk.
Incubation period (from date of exposure to first signs)	14 to 28 (commonly 18) days.	2 to 5 days.
Period of communicability (time when disease is contagious)	Not certain. From about 4 to 7 days before symptoms until swelling of salivary glands subsides.	During period of incubation and illness (about 10 days).
Most susceptible ages	Children and young people.	All ages.
Seasons of prevalence	Winter and spring.	Late winter and spring.
Prevention	None.	None.
Control	Isolation until swelling subsides. No attempt should be made to protect boys from this disease before they reach puberty. Immunity usual after one attack, but second attacks can occur.	Isolation until recovery. Use of antibiotics. One attack does not necessarily give immunity.

SMALLPOX	TETANUS	WHOOPING COUGH
A virus: present in skin pocks and discharges from mouth, nose, throat, bowels, bladder of infected people.	Tetanus bacillus: present in a wound so infected.	Pertussis bacillus: present in secretions from mouth and nose of infected people.
Contact with infected people or articles used by them.	Through soil, street dust, or articles contaminated with the bacillus.	Contact with infected people and articles used by them.
8 to 21 (commonly 12) days.	1 to 21 days. Sometimes longer. Commonly 8 to 12 days.	About 5 to 21 (commonly 10) days.
From first symptoms to disappearance of pocks.	Not communicable from person to person.	From onset of first symptoms to about 4th week of the disease.
All ages.	All ages.	Under 7 years.
Winter.	Summer.	Late winter and early spring.
Vaccination.	Inoculation with tetanus toxoid (in triple or quadruple vaccine for babies).	Inoculation with whooping cough vaccine (in triple or quadruple vaccine for babies).
Isolation until all pocks are gone. Immunity usual after one attack.	Booster dose of tetanus toxoid for protection after a wound. Antitoxin used in treatment and for temporary protection for child not immunized. One attack does not give immunity.	Special shots can lighten attack or give protection after exposure. Isolation for about 3 weeks from onset of spasmodic cough. Immunity usual after one attack.

Appendix II

READING MATERIALS

Many reliable organizations and agencies publish or distribute booklets useful to parents. You may want to write to any of the following for lists of their current materials:

American Medical Association
535 North Dearborn Street, Chicago 10, Ill.

American Social Health Association
1790 Broadway, New York 19, N.Y.

Association for Family Living
32 West Randolph Street, Chicago 1, Ill.

Child Study Association of America, Inc.
9 East 89th Street, New York 28, N.Y.

Child Welfare League of America, Inc.
44 East 23rd Street, New York 10, N.Y.

Children's Bureau
United States Department of Health, Education,
  and Welfare
Washington 25, D.C.

Family Service Association of America
215 Park Avenue South, New York 3, N.Y.

Mental Health Materials Center
104 East 25th Street, New York 10, N.Y.

Metropolitan Life Insurance Company
Health and Welfare Division
1 Madison Avenue, New York 10, N.Y.

National Association for Mental Health
10 Columbus Circle, New York 19, N.Y.

National Congress of Parents and Teachers
700 North Rush Street, Chicago 11, Ill.

National Recreation Association
8 West 8th Street, New York 11, N.Y.

Play Schools Association, Inc.
120 West 57th Street, New York 19, N.Y.

Public Affairs Committee, Inc.
22 East 38th Street, New York 16, N.Y.

Science Research Associates, Inc.
259 East Erie Street, Chicago 11, Ill.

Index

190